# Transformed by Worship

## The *Tarbiya* Effects of Ritual Worship in Islam

# TRANSFORMED BY WORSHIP

## The *Tarbiya* Effects of Ritual Worship in Islam

By Dr. Salah Soltan

Translated by
Abdelminem Mustafa

with Maha Ezzeddine and
Rayhan El-Alami

MAS Publishing
Washington, DC

712 H Street NE, Suite 1258
Washington, DC 20002
www.muslimamericansociety.org



Published by MAS Publishing, Washington DC

Interior design by Abdassamad Clarke
Printed in the U.S.A.

ISBN 978-1-7334527-1-7

*In the name of Allah,*
*the Most Compassionate, Most Merciful*

## MAS Mission

"To move people to strive for God-consciousness, liberty, and justice; and to convey Islam with utmost clarity."

# Contents

# Introduction

*All praise and thanks is to Allah, who created human beings in the most perfect state and revealed laws that raise them to their potential while protecting against pitfalls.*

*May blessings and peace be upon our Prophet Muhammad, the first of the worshippers, leader of the first and last generations; Peace upon his family, his pure and righteous companions, and those who follow earnestly in their footsteps until the Final Day.*

In this age of convenience and comfort, where material ease abounds, we are somehow always exhausted by the pursuit of the newest and latest. Our societies, east and west, are afflicted with an ailing global culture. While we scratch our every itch and gratify our cravings in an instant, humanity as a whole continues to suffer. Our bodies stay full while our souls starve. Every time we indulge a passing desire, our self-control diminishes. Our hearts harden, our characters change, and we become the enemy of our own souls, inviting destructive habits and slipping further down the slope of regression.

The concept that the human being is the nucleus for positive change and betterment in the world is pivotal to human outlook. This "change from within" concept is widespread in world philosophies and major religious doctrines. But all of these doctrines are afflicted with deficiencies in belief and implementation. Islam remains the one faultless measure, preserved unblemished as God's message, and the only perfect religion on this earth, as God stated in the Quran:

﴿إِنَّ ٱلدِّينَ عِندَ ٱللَّهِ ٱلْإِسْلَٰمُ ۗ وَمَا ٱخْتَلَفَ ٱلَّذِينَ أُوتُوا۟ ٱلْكِتَٰبَ إِلَّا مِنۢ بَعْدِ مَا جَآءَهُمُ ٱلْعِلْمُ بَغْيًۢا بَيْنَهُمْ ۗ وَمَن يَكْفُرْ بِـَٔايَٰتِ ٱللَّهِ فَإِنَّ ٱللَّهَ سَرِيعُ ٱلْحِسَابِ﴾

*True Religion, in God's eyes, is Islam. Those who were given the Scripture disagreed out of rivalry, only after they had been given knowledge—if anyone denies God's revelations, God is swift to take account.* [3:19]

God is the One who created the laws of the universe and legislated the laws in our religion. He revealed the scriptures and inspired the Prophet ﷺ to always do what is right. The One who designed the true religion is the same Creator who knows our inner and outer selves so intimately.

﴿أَلَا يَعْلَمُ مَنْ خَلَقَ وَهُوَ ٱللَّطِيفُ ٱلْخَبِيرُ﴾

*How could He who created not know His own creation, when He is the Most Subtle, the All-Aware.* [67:14]

Our Lord, who knows well every human desire, need, and personality, gave us the religion of Islam to live by. He understands our deepest longing for happiness in this life and the next.

Discovering the truths behind the rulings and the constants in faith can strengthen our confidence and conviction. Knowledge of the foundational principles within Islam leads to an understanding that there is a unity, organization, and sensible balance suited to every human being who seeks true contentment. That restoration of balance and contentment is not only desirable, but necessary. Every man and woman invested in the wellbeing of their people should take a careful look at today's reality; Islam offers healing for the dilemmas of country and community. God is fully capable of restoring vibrancy to human life, here in the 21st century.

The potential in human beings must be formed with balance—only then will we be empowered to develop a civilization and culture on earth in which the body and soul thrive together. Our morality would not conflict with material progress. There would be a harmony of hearts and minds, individuals and collectives, and religion and political authority. *Transformed by Worship* explores the many ways in which ritual worship (*'ibādah*), impacts human life. This work is translated from the Arabic *al-Āthar At-Tarbawiyyah lil-'Ibadāt fil-Islām* (The *Tarbiya* Effects of Ritual Worship in Islam), published in 2000. *Tarbiya* is the holistic nurturing and development of the human being.

In His mercy and care for us, God designed ritual worship to be a source of benefit and a source of *tarbiya*, shaping our identity and instilling elements essential to our personal and collective growth. Ignorance of the transformative aspect of worship has resulted in negative consequences for us as individuals and a community. Some of these negative results include:

**A disproportionate emphasis on the technicalities of worship.** There is much discussion about the *fiqh* rulings and obligation of worship. So often we elaborate on the do's and don'ts of the acts of worship without exploring the wisdom, secrets, and layers of meaning within worship. Each type of worship should have transformative effects on our person, a practical imprint on our lives. While the rulings are certainly important, neglecting the transformative nature of worship results in empty rituals that may be technically correct, but in spirit are dry and detached.

**Contradictions in character.** When worship is performed perfectly in terms of its requirements but with no attention to the holistic effects of that worship, contradictions in character begin to appear. A worshipper focuses on achieving ritual purity before prayer without washing the heart from envy and malice. He races to perform prayer on time but comes to work late in the morning. A manager makes sure to pay her zakah in full, but her employees are underpaid and exploited. A father makes Hajj and Umrah multiple times without considering the moral impact of leaving his family, neighbors, and local responsibilities. These inconsistencies in character and principles drive us away from practicing Islam and shake our confidence in Muslims, making the path of calling to Islam bumpy and uneven. Some sincere workers are forced to make counterintuitive excuses like, "Look at what Islam says, not what Muslims do." Contradictions in character among Muslims force us to make such embarrassing arguments.

**A lack of balance.** The nature and goals of worship

should inspire us in how we design programs and strategies for Islamic education and *tarbiya*. Areas of human growth and education cannot be compartmentalized. Social norms tend to isolate academic, physical, moral, and religious development. It is no small mistake to separate these fields from each other; there must be an overlap between them in order to nurture and shape the balanced Islamic personality. The global Muslim community, the *Ummah*, suffers from immaturity and an identity crisis due to this flawed model of separation.

By the *tarbiya* effects of worship, we mean the holistic developmental results: moral, spiritual, physical and intellectual, on the people who perform acts of worship in their comprehensive spirit. Although worship has many different forms, *Transformed by Worship* focuses specifically on five core elements of worship: ritual purification (*ṭahārah*), prayer (*ṣalāh*), Zakah, fasting (*ṣawm*), and Hajj. Worship is a purifying, nurturing, and transforming force in the life of the Muslim. It has powerful and practical effects on the following four components of human life:

1. **The Soul:** From our spiritual core emanates either true contentment or downheartedness. It represents the bond between us, the worshipper, and our Lord. This metaphysical component is very much intertwined with the next three aspects.
2. **Character:** It is the driving force behind either noble actions or vulgar behavior, lofty principles or

corruption, and tempered ambition or insatiable appetite.

3. **The Mind:** Intellect has the power to construct advanced civilizations or destroy centuries of progress. It either enhances good or cripples it, and has the potential to either increase the earth in bounty or leave it scorched and ruined.
4. **The Body:** Our bodies are the living containers that hold our souls. The physical component includes the intellect, and every ability and activity depends on the body's physical energy. Far-reaching dreams can be limited by feeble health. Those who have high ambitions must nurture and tend to their physical wellbeing as they develop the earth and convey goodness to its distant corners.

## A comprehensive understanding of worship

The term *'ibādāt* (ritual acts of worship) is the counterpart of *mu'āmalāt* (dealings) in the *shariah* (the Islamic teachings—commandments, guidance, and principles—that God addressed to mankind through Prophet Muhammad [1]ﷺ). *'Ibādāt* is a term prevalent in Islamic *fiqh*[2] and is understood to encompass the ritual acts of worship: ritual purification or *ṭaharah*, prayer, Zakah, fasting and Hajj, as well as other

1 [**Translator's note**]: The notation ﷺ means "May God's peace and blessings be upon him," which Muslims say whenever Prophet Muhammad's name is mentioned or written.

2 [**Translator's note**]: *Fiqh* can be defined as the human attempt to understand and codify the shariah.

forms of worship. The field of *fiqh* traditionally separates the two categories of worship and daily dealings for reasons of codification and practicality.

Outside the context of *fiqh*, however, it is important to understand that this separation limits our understanding of the broad scope of worship. The concept of worship should not be confined only to the few ritual acts we perform every day, as understood by secular and modernist ideals. We must insist on a comprehensive understanding of worship—it is, after all, the very reason God placed us on this earth.

Ibn Taymiyah, an eminent scholar from the 13th century, defines worship as follows: "Worship is everything beloved and pleasing to God, in speech and actions, public and private, external and internal." Worship includes belief and character. It includes purifying your character and strengthening your tenets of belief. It includes the process of self-development and rectifying the imbalances and injustices around us. It includes adhering to the *shariah*, the system of Islamic laws and rulings. Worship is a sweeping concept that can encompass the entire content and essence of human life, including all of our daily dealings and ritual worship. This understanding changes the lens through which we as Muslims look at our lives, as everything becomes an opportunity to please God.

Though the concept of worship is global, *Transformed by Worship* limits its focus to the set of familiar, foundational acts of worship that every Muslim engages with on a regular basis: ritual purification, prayer, Zakah, fasting, and

Hajj. Understanding the holistic impact and transformative nature of our customary, ritual acts of worship increases our gratitude to the One we worship; gratitude for His assigning these very specific forms of worship to us. As I researched and wrote this book, ritual worship transformed in my eyes from a religious requirement to a source of honor, favor, and great benefit from my Lord. I hope that readers journeying through this book experience the same shift, graduating from striving in worship to loving to worship.

To demonstrate this effect, here are a few examples, before diving deeper within the chapters of this book. We know very well that ritual purification is required for prayer and making *tawaf* around the Kaaba. Performing *wuḍu'* multiple times throughout the day is a matter of course for all Muslims, for the *asḥāb al-yameen*, or companions of the right, as described in Surah Al-Waqiah. But there is another level of worship and awareness, that of *al-muqarraboon*, those nearest to God. These are people who comprehend the beauty, transformation, and significance of worship. They cannot eat, enjoying the blessings of God, without *wuḍu'*, nor are they comfortable reading, writing, or studying without being in a state of purity. They even prefer to make *wuḍu'* before exercise!

It is similar with prayer. The five daily prayers are required of all Muslims, the companions of the right. There is no excuse to not pray, nor is there any religious mandate to exceed that requirement. But those nearest to God, who crave worshipping Him, cannot survive the night without spending time in His presence and calling upon Him. The length of time between the dawn prayer and the noon prayer feels too long to go without ritual worship, and so this believer prays the *ḍuha* prayer in the hours between sunrise and noon. They pray when they are confused, and they pray when they are worried. When their newborn child is born, not only do they pray out of excitement and gratitude, but they even make the call to prayer in the ear of their child so as to make it the first thing the child hears. Then when this lover of prayer passes away, we send them off with prayer.

Fasting and Zakah also take on different forms when we perform them while recognizing their transformative and rejuvenating nature, seeking through them to reach a higher degree. We know the basic requirements of fasting in Ramadan and paying a percentage of our wealth in Zakah every year. Those attached to God's worship feel a need for more than the basic requirement of fasting in Ramadan, and fast frequently throughout the year: Mondays, Thursdays, the three white days of every month, the days of Dhul Hijjah, perhaps even reaching the maximum Fast of Prophet David, which is to fast every other day all year long.

These believers also surpass the baseline requirements of Zakah, giving away their best quality clothing and food instead of just the minimum percentage of yearly savings. They look to all possible forms of spending for the sake of God beyond just money: they are generous with their time, energy, skills, and knowledge. The spirit of their lifestyle is open-handed, kind-hearted, and self-sacrificing. When times are hard, they ramp up their generosity, knowing the reforming effects and positive returns of charity, even though it means cutting back in the short term. The more desperate they are, the more these generous people spend, and they give in secret more than they give in public. Unlike others, they do not give away for the sake of decluttering their homes from whatever is old and unwanted; they search their souls for what they love the most in this life and share it. They live by the Prophet's saying: *"Whoever gives even a date's worth of charity that was earned by good and pure means—and God only accepts that which is good and pure—God will accept it with His right hand. Then He causes it to grow for whoever gave it, just as one of you would nurture his young horse until it becomes like a mountain."*[1]

One of the greatest effects of worship is an increase in our longing for The Lord of Strength and Honor. Through worship, the heart learns how to delight in its consciousness and presence before God, calling out to its creator with a deep yearning for Him. The heart is, in reality, suspended between the heavens and the earth. It calls out to its Lord, longing for His closeness and care, eager to meet Him, but also doubting its own worthiness and qualification for God's acceptance. The pure heart constantly asks itself: "Have I done enough for my Lord?" This is how we view the acts of worship, through a holistic and transformative lens: we look at its effects on the soul, character, mind and body. And when our analysis is sincere and true, it will result in our hearts breaking through the confines of our chest and reaching for the throne of God.

The methods used in this research include extrapolating

1 *Sahih al-Bukhari:* The Book on Zakah, "Charity from Wholesome Wealth," #1410

from the texts of the Qur'an and Sunnah, examining the fiqh rulings of the five pillars of worship, and reflecting on the impact of these forms worship on the soul, character, mind, and body. Through this approach, the most meaningful aspects of *tarbiya* within these acts of worship come to light. It is my hope that readers will understand through this study the transformative nature of worship, and see how it shapes our *tarbiya* through its effects on our mindfulness and love for God; our treatment of other people and creation; how we explore, innovate, and learn; and how we nurture our bodies. By implementing this concept of transformative worship, we can live a life that is God-centered, vibrant, and noble.

# Part I

# The Soul

Purification Prayer Zakah Fasting Hajj

# Purification

Among the amazing aspects of Islam is that physical purification is mandatory, guiding the Muslim to reach an intrinsic purity by fulfilling an act of worship, in addition to the requirement of external cleanliness. Purifying oneself from every form of filth is a rite of worship in itself with resounding effects on the soul's wellbeing. The great Muslim scholar of philosophy and spirituality Abu Ḥamid al-Ghazāli points out, "The most pressing matter is the secret, inner purification, as it is impossible when the Prophet ﷺ said, *'Purity is one half of faith,'*[1] that he meant to focus on cleaning the body with water and soap while polluting one's soul and leaving it filled with filth and corruption."

Al-Ghazali mentioned that there are four levels of purification: purifying the body from impurities, purifying the limbs from sins, purifying the heart from reprehensible behaviors and vices, and purifying one's inner focus from everything but God. This highest level of purity is attained by the Prophets and the individuals who embodied the Truth (*ṣiddeeqoon*).[2]

1 Muslim, *Sahih Muslim*: The Book on Purification, "The Virtues of *Wuḍu*"' (Narrated by Abu Malik al-Ash'ari)

2 Al-Ghazāli, *Iḥyā' 'Uloom ad-Deen,* v.1, pp. 125-126

## PURIFICATION IS A MEANS TO GOD'S LOVE

With physical and spiritual purity, those who purify themselves earn God's love. God says,

﴿فِيهِ رِجَالٌ يُحِبُّونَ أَن يَتَطَهَّرُوا۟ وَٱللَّهُ يُحِبُّ ٱلْمُطَّهِّرِينَ﴾

*In it are men who love to be purified.*
*And Allah loves those who purify themselves.* [9:108]

This love from God for His servants brings a sense of clarity and etherealness to their souls. This lightness of soul, resulting from physical purification and God's love, is a comfort within the chests, a relief from anxiety, a gratification of spirit, and a delight within the heart.

## WUDU' WASHES AWAY SIN

*Wuḍu'* is the basic ritual of purification in Islam, performed before acts of worship, and involves washing the hands, mouth, nostrils, face, arms, head and feet with water. Performing the act of *wuḍu'* brings the soul back to a state of purity from the sins that it has committed. This is mentioned in the narration collected by Malik, an-Nasa'i, and Ibn Majah, and reported by the companion Abdullah as-Sunabihi wherein the Prophet ﷺ said, "*When a believing servant makes wuḍu' and rinses his mouth, wrongdoings leave from his mouth; and when he rinses his nose, wrongdoings leave from his nose; and when he washes his face, wrongdoings leave from his face, even emerging from under his eyelids. Then when he washes his hands, the wrongdoings leave from his hands, even emerging from under his fingernails; and when he wipes his head, the wrongdoings leave from his head, even emerging from his ears; and when he washes his feet, wrongdoings leave from his feet, even emerging from under his toenails. His walk to the mosque and his prayer are then additional rewards for him.*"[1] Furthermore, al-Bukhari and Muslim report from Uthman bin Affan that the Messenger of Allah ﷺ said, "*Never does a Muslim person make wuḍu', striving for excellence therein, and then prays a prayer except that he is forgiven for whatever is between that prayer and the one that follows it.*"[2] Thus we see that the act of *wuḍu'* can be a means for the soul to return to being pure, like a stained garment becoming clean and bright again after being washed.

## Purification inspires remembrance

The link between acts of ritual purification and the heart-warming, soul-soothing remembrance of God is made clear in many hadiths. Imam Muslim reports with a chain from Anas bin Malik that whenever the Prophet ﷺ would enter the washroom, he would say, "*Allah, I take refuge with you from all evil and filthy things*" (*Allāhumma innee a'oodhu bika min al-khubthi wal-khabā'ith*).[3] When he exited the bathroom, he would then rush to remember God, saying, "*Your forgiveness!*" (*ghufrānak*) or "*All praise be to God who cleansed me of filth and kept me healthy*" (*al-ḥamdu lillāh il-ladhi adh-haba 'anni al-adhā wa'āfāni*).

1 Malik, *al-Muwaṭṭa':* The Book on Purification, "The *Wuḍu'* Collection" v. 1 p. 31; an-Nasa'i, *Sunan an-Nasa'i*: The Book on Purification

2 Al-Bukhari, *Sahih al-Bukhari:* The Book on Wuḍu', "*Wuḍu'* in Repetitions of Threes"; Muslim, *Sahih Muslim:* The Book on Purification, "The Virtue of Praying Immediately after Making *Wuḍu'*"

3 Muslim, *Sahih Muslim*: The Book on Menstruation

In another hadith collected by Imam Ahmad and Ibn Majah with a chain from Abu Hurayrah, the Prophet ﷺ said, *"There is no prayer for anyone who is not in a state of wuḍu', and there is no wuḍu' for anyone who does not remember God thereupon."*[1] Imam Muslim reports with a chain from Umar bin al-Khattab (may God be pleased with him) that the Prophet ﷺ said, *"There is not a single person among you who makes wuḍu'—doing so thoroughly—and then says, 'I testify that there is nothing worthy of worship but God, alone, without any partners, and I testify that Muhammad is His servant and messenger,' except that the eight doors to Paradise are opened for him to enter from any of them he wishes."*[2] This immense reward for what seems to be simple words of prayer should be seen as low-hanging fruit, and any sound-minded individual would focus their efforts to harvest it. Yet these rewards will not be reached by the one who is unmindful, who is made by Satan to be heedless of God's remembrance, thereby causing his heart to harden, his soul to weaken, and his chest to fill with worry, grief, and distress. This heedless individual will sink from joy to misery, and will have no peace of mind, regardless of his worldly efforts, unless he returns to God—the Exalted—in remembrance of Him with his heart, his soul, his limbs, and his tongue.

1 Ibn Majah, *Sunan Ibn Majah:* The Book on Purification, "Saying *'Bismillah'* when Performing *Wuḍu',*" #390

2 Muslim, *Sahih Muslim:* The Book on Purification, "Recommended Words of Prayer after Performing *Wuḍu';*" at-Tirmidhi adds to this: *"Allah, make me one of the oft-repenting, and make me one of those who strive for purity"* (*Allāhumm aj'alnee min at-tawwābeen waj'alnee min al-mutaṭahhireen*).

### Purification emits light

Purity is one of the signs by which the believers will be recognized on the Day of Judgement. Without it, the believers and disbelievers would look the same on the Day of Judgement, but washing oneself and performing *wuḍu'* will summon a glowing light to the face, hands, and feet through which the righteous will be distinguished from those who will be dark and gloomy. Al-Bukhari and Muslim both report that the Prophet ﷺ said, *"You will be the ones who will be shining from the heads and limbs on the Day of Judgement from making wuḍu' thoroughly. So anyone with the capability among you should then extend the shining of his head and limbs!"*[1] The long shining marks on the heads and limbs will be glowing indicators, radiating light on the Day of Judgement. This is also how the intercession of the Prophet ﷺ will be attained on the Day of Judgement.

### Purification even for the deceased

A major sign that purifying the body is linked to purifying the soul is that the act of purification is not limited to the living; it is our duty to wash even the dead! Imam al-Kāsāni, a Hanafi scholar of Islamic Law, said that washing the deceased "has been a duty from our Prophet Adam until this very day."[2] The prolific Andalusian scholar and polymath Ibn Hazm said, "Washing each deceased

1 This is a chapter in and of itself: "Extending the Shining of the Head and Limbs."

2 *Badā'i' aṣ-Ṣanā'i'*, vol. 1, p. 299; for more on this, see *Kitāb an-Nayl,* Muhammad bin Yusuf Aṭṭafayyish, v. 2, p. 217 and *al-Fiqh,* Muhammad al-Husaini ash-Shirāzi, v. 12, p. 299.

Muslim is an absolute obligation. Even if he has already been buried without being washed, he must be dug up."[1] This emphasis on being cleansed at death is due to the fact that the deceased is moving forward to God. No Muslim can escape this reality, and so anyone who is coming before Him should present themselves in the most beautiful image with the utmost purity.

There is, however, one exception, wherein the deceased is cleansed through an action rather than with water, and through sacrifice rather than through being washed: the martyr. This is someone who offered their soul exclusively to Allah, hoping for martyrdom, wishing desperately for Allah's mercy, Paradise, and His pleasure. Even if a martyr is covered in blood, he is not to be washed. Though blood is usually counted as an impure substance, all of that falls to the wayside in the face of this metaphysical purification through which the martyr arrives at their Lord. There is no need to wash the bodies of martyrs, and they are to be buried as they were killed.[2] They will meet their Lord covered in the color of blood, but exuding the scent of musk. Allah will boast of them to His servants that these are the martyrs who offered up their own souls and wealth for Allah.

### Purification is a lesson in submission

Many rules of the ritual acts of purification are meant to teach submission to God's command without hesitation. Even if your mind cannot ascertain the wisdom of a specific

1 Ibn Hazm, *al-Muḥalla*, vol. 2, p. 22

2 Ibn Qudāmah, *al-Kāfī*, v. 1, pp. 247, 253; Aṭṭafayyish, *Sharḥ Kitāb an-Nayl*, v. 2, p. 219

act, your heart must submit because it is the truth and is the ultimate good. For instance, someone who cannot find any water must perform the act of *tayammum*. At face value, it seems like nothing more than rubbing earthly soil on only some of the limbs involved in *wuḍu'*, but it is an act of purification nonetheless and even suffices someone from having to wash their whole body after being in a state of major ritual impurity (*janābah*). When Ammar bin Yasir encountered this issue of being in a state of major ritual impurity in the absence of water, he rationally came to the conclusion that he must perform *tayammum* by rolling around in the soil to suffice for washing his whole body with water. But he was mistaken—this extra measure was uncalled for. *Tayammum* is meant to be purely a matter of worship through which one's submission to Allah is expressed. It is an expression of trust and certainty, and a sign that one's heart is free from the satanic whispers that cause some to only comply with what their intellect can rationalize and that which their heart is comfortable.

This lesson can also be seen in other rulings regarding purification: in wiping over the top of your socks during *wuḍu'*, and not the bottom; in the seemingly adventitious status of purity for some types of water over others; and in the requirement for making *wuḍu'* after flatulence, urination, defecation, and the secretion of pre-seminal fluid while a complete washing of the whole body (*ghusl*) is required for the secretion of semen. Semen is technically less impure than feces, but we pay deference to God's knowledge over all else. In ritual acts of purification, we journey from insisting on certainty of the intellect to striving for the submission of our hearts. By observing and pondering over God's majestic universe, the subtleties of the world's inner-workings, and the miracle of the Qur'an, we come to the reassuring conclusion that we must submit in theory and practice to any part of the scripture that is confirmed to be authentic.

## Prayer

Prayer (*ṣalāh*) is a mobilizing force in the life of the Muslim, a ritual by which life and the heart are set aright. It renders the soul pure and restores its heavenly essence, releasing it from the misery and perverseness of disobedience and sin. It opens an intimate path to confiding in God, most High, and perfecting the connection to Him. The effects on the soul are profound and innumerable.

### Prayer nurtures the soul

Prayer is our spiritual workout. We can never feel contentment in our hearts if we satiate our bodies while starving our souls. Our materialistic culture has eased everything for the body, paving the way for its every comfort, delight, and beautification. At the same time, it has advanced a generation of tight chests, unstable psyches, empty hearts, and turbulent souls. It has produced a people who are uncomfortable with their own selves due to the imbalance of our overfed bodies and starving souls. We now see a spread of mental and social pathologies, diseases and complications, not the least of which is the rise of suicide and violent killings. Many have resorted to living a life without meaning or purpose, numbed to any profound spiritual feeling in their heart.

Prayer creates for the believer an assured heart, a percipient soul, and a balanced self. It wipes away our shortcomings so that our conscience is at ease and not overburdened by its own guilt, by the will of Allah. In this way we understand what is narrated by Imam Ahmad in his *Musnad* that Abdullah bin Muhammad bin Al-Hanafiyyah said, "I visited with Abu Bakr a relative of ours from the Ansar, and the time of prayer entered. He said: 'Bring me some water to make *wuḍu'* so that I may pray and find relief.' He saw our surprise at his manner of speaking, so he explained that he heard Allah's Prophet ﷺ say: '*Rise, Bilal, and relieve us with the prayer.*'"[1] In an alternative narration, also cited in Imam Ahmad's *Musnad*, Hudhayfa bin Al-Yaman said, "If Allah's Prophet ﷺ was distressed about something he would pray."[2] Prayer should be the rich oasis where we find relaxation and enjoyment. Prayer is where we experience the company of God and quench our hearts with the love of The Exalted. This sanctuary of prayer is what bolsters our certainty in God's justice. It makes us hungry for His favor, hopeful in his Mercy, and never despairing of His forebearance and grace - just as God, the Exalted, says:

﴿الَّذِينَ آمَنُوا وَتَطْمَئِنُّ قُلُوبُهُم بِذِكْرِ اللَّهِ أَلَا بِذِكْرِ اللَّهِ تَطْمَئِنُّ الْقُلُوبُ﴾

1 *Al-Musnad,* v. 5, p. 371

2 *Al-Musnad* v. 5, p. 377

*Those who have faith and whose hearts find peace in the remembrance of God— truly it is in the remembrance of God that hearts find peace.* [13: 28]

## An unmatched joy

Being consistent in your prayers builds an attachment in the heart for standing in the presence of your Lord. Prayer becomes a true delight that will move you to surpass even your own expectations of yourself. You will not only find ease in praying the five daily required prayers, but even eagerly look for every opportunity to perform extra prayers. What others on the outside see as the hardship or inconvenience of prayer will be seen as opportunities for deep mindfulness, loving pleas, and tasting the sweetness of faith.

These experiences become so ingrained that you will wake up in the middle of the night eager to taste the sweetness of prayer, yearning deeply to meet your Lord. It is an unparalleled bliss that will draw you from the warm comfort of your bed. And if you ever miss that nightly appointment, your day will not be the same; it would be filled with the remorse of having slept through a meeting with your Lord. That is true vitality in the heart and purity of the soul for a believer. This is what is alluded to when God, The Exalted, describes those who pray their night prayers consistently:

﴿تَتَجَافَىٰ جُنُوبُهُمْ عَنِ الْمَضَاجِعِ يَدْعُونَ رَبَّهُمْ خَوْفًا
وَطَمَعًا وَمِمَّا رَزَقْنَاهُمْ يُنفِقُونَ * فَلَا تَعْلَمُ نَفْسٌ مَّا
أُخْفِيَ لَهُم مِّن قُرَّةِ أَعْيُنٍ جَزَاءً بِمَا كَانُوا يَعْمَلُونَ﴾

> *Their sides shun their beds in order to pray to their Lord in fear and hope; they give to others some of what We have given them. No soul knows what joy is kept hidden in store for them as a reward for what they have done.*
> [32:16-17]

### Prayer provides direction

Prayer protects our souls from fragmentation and our hearts from being torn between the glamor of our world and the principles of the heavens. Consider all of the different supplications you make when you stand to pray. You start by purifying your intention: "*I have turned my face in pure faith towards the One who originated the skies and the earth, submissively, and I am surely not among those who associate partners with God.*" Then when you bow, you remember Allah: "*God, for you I have bowed, and in you I have believed, and to you I have submitted. Humbled is my hearing, my sight, my mind, my bones, my blood, and every step my foot has taken before God, Lord of the Worlds.*" When you prostrate you say, "*My face prostrates to the One that created it and fashioned it and portioned its hearing and seeing therein—blessings are to God, the most perfect of any creator!*" With every utterance, you reestablish the primacy of God above all things that may be tearing you away from Him.

The Quran describes the one who is swept away by temptation and trial as someone disoriented, tempted by devils into the wilderness, though his companions call out to him in guidance. Such individuals hold mundane, earthly aspirations, some which they may achieve and others, unattainable, over which they anguish and grieve.

This is the fragmentation and tearing of the self, which God describes,

وَاعْلَمُوا أَنَّ اللَّهَ يَحُولُ بَيْنَ الْمَرْءِ وَقَلْبِهِ وَأَنَّهُ إِلَيْهِ تُحْشَرُونَ

*Know that God comes between a man and his heart, and that you will be gathered to Him. [8:24]*

This is the bitter reality for millions of people, who will not feel whole or complete without the experience of standing in prayer before their Lord.

## PRAYER IS REASSURANCE

It is the nature of prayer, when performed correctly with attention and sincerity, to transform into a lifestyle. One of the results of fully engaging with prayer is that it will become your anchor. When you encounter difficulties, you will relieve your distress with prayer, and when you are conflicted in a matter, you will solve it by praying *Ṣalāh Al-Istikhārah.*[1] You will walk away from your prayer feeling confident in the best choice that God makes for you. Then if this difficulty intensifies, you will hurry to perform *Ṣalāh Al-Ḥājah.* Imam at-Tirmidhi narrated that, according to Abdur-Rahman bin Abdullah bin Abu 'Awf, the Prophet of Allah ﷺ said: "*Whoever has a need from God or from any of the children of Adam, let him make wuḍu'—and he should perfect his wuḍu'—and then pray two rakahs. Then he should praise God, the Exalted, and send blessings upon the Prophet ﷺ and say, 'There is nothing worthy of worship but God the Knowing, the Forbearing, the*

1 [**Translator's Note**]: This is a voluntary prayer one can perform when making a decision.

*Generous—exalted above all imperfections is God, Lord of the grand throne! All praise and gratitude is due to God, Lord of all creation! I ask you for what ensures your mercy and invites your forgiveness, and to gain from every goodness, and to be saved from every sin. Do not leave any mistake of mine except that you have forgiven it, or worry except that you have lifted it, or matter which pleases you except that you have ordained it—most Merciful, always Merciful!*’[1]

This sincere supplication of need relieves difficulty, soothes worries, and comforts the heart. Consider how corrupted people rush to their defective outlets when they are overwhelmed with pressure; they drown out their concerns with loud music, intoxicants, and other surface level treatments for deeply rooted problems. No matter how delightful the euphemisms used for these may sound, they are ultimately tools of destruction, both physically and spiritually. They destroy the human psyche, as they deceive us to think that a cure can be found in a toxin, only adding layers of grief and sorrow.

Prayer, on the other hand, is a method of keeping the heart alive and the soul light, so that even if the Muslim commits a serious wrongdoing, or is on the verge of sin, he rushes to a humble prayer that removes that black blemish from his heart. There is in our tradition a prayer known as the Prayer of Repentance. Imam Ibn Majah narrates in his *Musnad*, on the authority of Abdullah bin Mas‘ood that a man once met a woman for a shameless act, but it did not reach the point of fornication. When he went to the Prophet ﷺ and confessed that to him, God, the Exalted, revealed:

1 *Sunan at-Tirmidhi:* The Witr Prayer, "The Prayer of Need," #477

﴿وَأَقِمِ الصَّلَاةَ طَرَفَيِ النَّهَارِ وَزُلَفًا مِّنَ اللَّيْلِ ۚ إِنَّ
الْحَسَنَاتِ يُذْهِبْنَ السَّيِّئَاتِ ۚ ذَٰلِكَ ذِكْرَىٰ لِلذَّاكِرِينَ﴾

*Keep up the prayer at both ends of the day, and during parts of the night, for good things drive bad away— this is a reminder for those who are aware* [11:114]

The man asked, "Messenger of Allah, is this intended for me?" The Prophet ﷺ said *"For whoever takes it."*[1] Ibn Majah reports from Ali bin Abu Talib in his *Musnad* that Abu Bakr narrated that the Prophet ﷺ said, *"There is not a Muslim who commits a sin, but then makes wuḍu', perfecting his wuḍu', and then prays two rakahs and repents to his Lord except that his Lord forgives him."*[2]

Prayer, then, is a purification for the heart that guarantees the return of one's conscience to its natural state. If one is plagued by guilt, worry, or indecision, prayer can be their solution. Most likely the best comparison given is what is narrated in Bukhari and Muslim: that prayer is like a river in which the Muslim bathes five times everyday, leaving no part of the body uncleansed. This hidden power of prayer is what moved surgeon, biologist, and Nobel laureate Alexis Carrel to write,:

> Prayer is a force as real as terrestrial gravity. As a physician, I have seen men, after all other therapy had failed, lifted out of disease and melancholy by the serene effort of prayer. It is the

1 *Sunan Ibn Majah: Establishing the Prayer,* "Prayer as an Expiation," #398

2 ibid., #395

> only power in the world that seems to overcome the so-called laws of nature; the occasions on which prayer has dramatically done this have been termed miracles. But a constant, quieter miracle takes place hourly in the hearts of men and women who have discovered that prayer supplies them with a steady flow of sustaining power in their daily lives… Prayer, like radium, is a source of luminous, self-generating energy… Human beings seek to augment their finite energy by addressing themselves to the Infinite Source of all energy. When we pray, we link ourselves with the inexhaustible motive power that spins the universe. We ask that a part of this power be apportioned to our needs. Even in asking, our human deficiencies are filled, and we arise strengthened and repaired.[1]

## Zakah

Giving Zakah has many preventative and restorative effects for the Muslim's soul. God created the human being in an ideal form, letting us live in the finest of dwellings and honoring us to the highest degree. But we human beings frequently disgrace ourselves to the lowest of levels, forgetting our role in the world and shirking our responsibilities. The foremost culprit in our descent is our excessive love for wealth.

1 Carrel, Alexis. "Prayer is Power." *The Reader's Digest.* (March 1963)

## Wealth is a means

The love for wealth is natural, and it is considered a blessing of God upon the human being, an incentive to develop the world around us. God, the Supreme, says about human beings,

﴿وَإِنَّهُۥ لِحُبِّ ٱلْخَيْرِ لَشَدِيدٌ﴾

*And they are truly extreme in their love of ⌐worldly¬ gains.* [100:8]

Excessiveness, however, leads to hoarding and an aversion to share with those in need. This is how many regress from being God-centered servants to being prisoners of this world and servants to their own desires. Al-Bukhari and Ibn Majah report that the Prophet ﷺ prayed against such people, saying, *"Doomed is the servant of this world! Doomed is the servant of the dirham! Doomed is the servant of the garment! If he is given, he rejoices, and if he is not given, he becomes angry. May he perish and never be saved! May he be pricked by a thorn and never be relieved!"*[1]

This doom described in the hadith is a misery of the soul and a darkness of the heart, as the love for wealth replaces the love for God. What was only a means of pursuing God's pleasure becomes an end in and of itself. Wealth was created to be a means of living through this world and building it up through development, providing many opportunities to please God. But when these means of amassing and hoarding wealth become ends in and of themselves, God's curse is earned. God, the Exalted, says:

1 *Sunan Ibn Majah:* The Book on Austerity, "Those Who Seek Abundance," #4136

﴿وَيْلٌ لِّكُلِّ هُمَزَةٍ لُّمَزَةٍ ۞ ٱلَّذِى جَمَعَ مَالًا وَعَدَّدَهُۥ ۞ يَحْسَبُ أَنَّ مَالَهُۥٓ أَخْلَدَهُۥ ۞ كَلَّا ۖ لَيُنۢبَذَنَّ فِى ٱلْحُطَمَةِ ۞ وَمَآ أَدْرَىٰكَ مَا ٱلْحُطَمَةُ﴾

*Woe to every backbiter, slanderer, who amasses wealth ⌜greedily⌝ and counts it ⌜repeatedly⌝, thinking that their wealth will make them immortal! Not at all! Such a person will certainly be tossed into the Crusher. And what will make you realize what the Crusher is?* [104:1-5]

Thus it is understood that giving Zakah safeguards the soul from this excessive love of wealth. It is protection from the negative effects of wealth, even though that wealth was obtained through permissible means. One of the greatest objectives of giving Zakah is mentioned by God when He says:

﴿خُذْ مِنْ أَمْوَٰلِهِمْ صَدَقَةً تُطَهِّرُهُمْ وَتُزَكِّيهِم بِهَا وَصَلِّ عَلَيْهِمْ ۖ إِنَّ صَلَوٰتَكَ سَكَنٌ لَّهُمْ﴾

*Take from their wealth ⌜O Prophet⌝ charity to purify them and bring about their growth, and pray for them—surely your prayer is a source of comfort for them.* [9:103]

Zakah, then, is purification and growth. It transforms us from the squalid state of worshipping wealth to the purity of the pious and sincere worshippers of God—those who, though they owned the world, held it in their hands, not in their hearts. They were happy to share their wealth generously, setting examples of gratitude and high expectation for the Muslims. They practiced the teachings of the Messenger of Allah ﷺ, when he said, *"How great is good wealth for a good servant!"*[1]

### The holistic impact of Zakah

The Hanafi scholar al-Kāsāni said about the impact of Zakah on the human soul:

> It purifies the soul from the captivity of sins, shapes its character through the observance of generosity and the purging of stinginess. Through the practice of Zakah, the soul becomes accustomed to benevolence and builds up the strength to do right by others and pay them their dues. It is also a form of gratitude to God for His blessings.[2]

### An antidote to greed

God says regarding the prevention of the disease of greed:

﴿وَمَن يُوقَ شُحَّ نَفْسِهِۦ فَأُوْلَٰٓئِكَ هُمُ ٱلْمُفْلِحُونَ﴾

*And whoever is saved from the selfishness of their own souls, it is they who are ⌜truly⌝ successful.* [64:16]

Success therefore hinges on being free of the malady of greed. Paying Zakah on the money that you save, your crops, your freely grazing livestock, and your business

1 Imam Ahmad, *Musnad al-Imam Ahmad*, v. 4, p. 197

2 *Badā'i' aṣ-Ṣanā'i'*, al-Kāsāni, v. 2, p. 3

inventory acts as a potent antidote. A charity is prescribed for each of the types of wealth that a person can be blessed with to prevent the infection of greed from creeping into the soul. Not only does this infection stop a Muslim from loving others and pleasing God, but it also prevents him from bliss in the afterlife.

Greed and selfishness draw the anger and wrath of God, earning a banishment from Paradise. The wealth that was supposed to be a means to secure goodness in this life and the next becomes a source of misery in this world, inciting a fixation on its pursuit, immoderation in saving, and an obsessive addiction to counting it. In the afterlife, this misery becomes pain through flames of fire or in the form of a poisonous snake, as described by the Prophet ﷺ when he said, *"Whoever receives wealth from God but does not pay its Zakah, his wealth will be transformed into a bald, poisonous, horned snake that will choke him on the Day of Resurrection. It will bite his cheeks and say, 'I am your wealth, I am your treasure.'"* Then he recited:[1]

﴿وَلَا يَحْسَبَنَّ ٱلَّذِينَ يَبْخَلُونَ بِمَآ ءَاتَىٰهُمُ ٱللَّهُ مِن فَضْلِهِۦ
هُوَ خَيْرًا لَّهُم بَلْ هُوَ شَرٌّ لَّهُمْ سَيُطَوَّقُونَ مَا بَخِلُوا۟ بِهِۦ
يَوْمَ ٱلْقِيَـٰمَةِ وَلِلَّهِ مِيرَٰثُ ٱلسَّمَـٰوَٰتِ وَٱلْأَرْضِ وَٱللَّهُ بِمَا
تَعْمَلُونَ خَبِيرٌ﴾

*And do not let those who ⌜greedily⌝ withhold Allah's bounties think it is good for them—in fact, it is bad*

1 Al-Bukhari, *Sahih al-Bukhari: Exegetical Commentary of the Qur'an*, "Surah 3, Verse 180," #4565, #1403 is similar

> *for them! They will be leashed ⌜by their necks⌝ on the Day of Judgment with whatever ⌜wealth⌝ they used to withhold. And Allah is the ⌜sole⌝ inheritor of the heavens and the earth. And Allah is All-Aware of what you do.* [3:180]

Al-Bukhari and Muslim also report that the Messenger of Allah ﷺ said, *"There is no owner of any herd of camels, cattle, or sheep who does not pay forth its Zakah except that it will come on the Day of Resurrection in its largest and fattest form, piercing him with its horns and trampling him with its hooves. Every time its hind legs pass, its forelegs come back on him until the people are judged."*[1]

## CHARITY'S TRUE VALUE

To contrast these dark threats is an inspiring description of those who pay Zakah and share their wealth, a description that fills the heart with hope and the soul with happiness for God's grace. God says:

﴿أَلَمْ يَعْلَمُوٓا۟ أَنَّ ٱللَّهَ هُوَ يَقْبَلُ ٱلتَّوْبَةَ عَنْ عِبَادِهِۦ وَيَأْخُذُ ٱلصَّدَقَٰتِ وَأَنَّ ٱللَّهَ هُوَ ٱلتَّوَّابُ ٱلرَّحِيمُ﴾

> *Do they not know that Allah alone accepts the repentance of His servants and receives ⌜their⌝ charity, and that Allah alone is the Accepter of Repentance, Most Merciful?* [9:108]

Additionally, al-Bukhari reports with a chain from Abu Hurayrah that the Prophet ﷺ said, *"Whoever gives even a*

1 Al-Bukhari, *Sahih al-Bukhari*, #6638; Muslim, *Sahih Muslim*, #990

*date's worth of charity that was earned by good and pure means—and God only accepts that which is good and pure—God will accept it with His right hand. Then He causes it to grow for whoever gave it, just as one of you would nurture his young horse until it becomes like a mountain."*[1]

There is no doubt that remembering God's mercy soothes the grief of the distressed, relieves the misery of the destitute, and alleviates the pain of the hungry and ill. When the companions of the Prophet ﷺ realized that the true value of wealth lay in spending it for God's pleasure, they raced each other to give to all kinds of good causes. Al- Wāqidi, Ibn Sa'd, and Ibn Kathir report, for example, that the companions competed with one another to contribute to the expenditures of fighting for God's cause in the Battle of Tabuk. The first to show up with a large load of wealth, carrying the entirety of what he owned, was Abu Bakr. Umar then brought half of his wealth, Abbas brought some of his, and now the competition was in full force! Talhah bin Ubaydullah brought his load of wealth, and Muhammad bin Maslamah brought his contribution. Abdulrahman bin Awf brought two hundred *uqiyyah.* Sa'd ibn Ubadah came forth with a generous contribution, and Asim ibn Adiy brought ninety barrels of dates. Uthman bin Affan initially sponsored a third of the army, and though he had already surpassed everyone else in his contribution, continued to sponsor more until he ensured that the army was adequately equipped. Some men brought camels,

1 *Sahih al-Bukhari:* The Book on Zakah, "Charity from Wholesome Wealth," #1410

assigning one camel to a pair of soldiers and having them take turns riding it. Even the women contributed as much as they could, filling the garment held out by the Messenger of Allah ﷺ with their bracelets, anklets, and rings.[1]

As-Suyooṭi reports from Aishah and 'Urwah bin Zubayr that on the day that Abu Bakr became Muslim, he had forty thousand dinars. He spent them all on the Messenger of Allah ﷺ, to the point that when he once entered the mosque and found someone begging, he went back to his house to find only a small piece of food in the hands of his son Abdulrahman. He took it away from him and gave it to the beggar.[2] Ibn al-Jawzi reports that Abu Bakr donated his most precious garden, which contained six hundred palm trees, when he heard the ayah:[3]

﴿وَأَقْرِضُوا۟ ٱللَّهَ قَرْضًا حَسَنًا﴾

*... and lend to Allah a good loan.* [73:20]

These scenes from the time of the companions show how each companion would give much more than what was required of them. This stems from a sincere faith wherein their love for Allah governed their heart and tempered their love for wealth. These are the models that every Muslim must follow.

1 Al-Wāqidi, *al-Maghāzī,* vol. 3, pp. 991-992; Ibn Sa'd, *aṭ-Ṭabaqāt al-Kubra,* v. 2, p. 238; Ibn Kathir, *al-Bidāyah wan-Nihāyah;* as-Suyooṭi, *Seerat al-Khulafā',* p. 234; Ibn al-Jawzi, *Ṣifat aṣ-Ṣafwah,* v. 1, p. 116

2 *Tāreekh al-Khulafā',* p. 77

3 *Ṣifat aṣ-Ṣafwah,* v. 2, pp. 252-253

### Zakah al-Fitr is purification and celebration

The ritual of Zakah al-Fiṭr, wherein every Muslim donates a specific amount of food to the needy at the end of Ramadan, carries a unique spiritual significance. It is described by the Prophet ﷺ, as Ibn Majah reports that he said, *"The obligation of Zakah al-Fiṭr is a source of purification for the idle speech and obscenities of the one who fasted, and a meal for the needy."*[1] So Zakah al-Fiṭr is a means of purification for the old and the young, the rich and the poor, and for men and women, as it is obligatory on everyone to spend on those beneath them. This form of Zakah purifies their souls, and it is clear that the purification here is not physical, but rather spiritual. In this spirit of giving, the entire community purifies their wealth and enters together upon their celebration of Eid.

## Fasting

Fasting has profound effects on the spiritual life of the Muslim individual. While opportunities for voluntary fasting are scattered through weekly and monthly regimens, the month of Ramadan is a concentrated dose of spirituality mandated for all Muslims.

### Fasting is training for taqwa

*Taqwa* is a consciousness and mindfulness of God, and it is a catalyst for self-improvement. When *taqwa* is practiced, a

1 Ibn Majah, *Sunan Ibn Majah:* The Book on Zakah, "The Fiṭr Alms," #1827 (narrated by Ibn Abbas)

contentment results within the soul that lightens the burdens of grief and fear. God, The Exalted, says in the Quran:

﴿فَمَنِ اتَّقَىٰ وَأَصْلَحَ فَلَا خَوْفٌ عَلَيْهِمْ وَلَا هُمْ يَحْزَنُونَ﴾

*Those who are conscious of God and live righteously, there will be no fear, nor will they grieve.* [7:35]

Fear and grief are the primary causes of anxiety. A heightened anxiety in the present is caused by fear of the future and grief over the past. By being conscious and mindful of God in the present moment, a Muslim is grounded by *taqwa*. It is the guide and handhold by which a Muslim navigates through unknown darkness and the turns of life. God says in the Quran:

﴿وَمَن يَتَّقِ اللَّهَ يَجْعَل لَّهُ مَخْرَجًا
وَيَرْزُقْهُ مِنْ حَيْثُ لَا يَحْتَسِبُ﴾

*God will find a way out for those who are mindful of Him, and will provide for them from an unexpected source…* [65:2-3]

So long as you are mindful of God, you are enfolded in His Guardianship and protection. God also says:

﴿أَلَا إِنَّ أَوْلِيَاءَ اللَّهِ لَا خَوْفٌ عَلَيْهِمْ وَلَا هُمْ يَحْزَنُونَ﴾

*But for those who are on God's side there is no fear, nor shall they grieve.* [10:62]

The impact of taqwa on our overall happiness in this life and in the next cannot be understated. It is enough to mention the peace of mind and tranquility enjoyed by those who were mindful of God, once they reached their final destination:

﴿إِنَّ ٱلْمُتَّقِينَ فِى مَقَامٍ أَمِينٍ * فِى جَنَّـٰتٍ وَعُيُونٍ *
يَلْبَسُونَ مِن سُندُسٍ وَإِسْتَبْرَقٍ مُّتَقَـٰبِلِينَ * كَذَٰلِكَ
وَزَوَّجْنَـٰهُم بِحُورٍ عِينٍ * يَدْعُونَ فِيهَا بِكُلِّ فَـٰكِهَةٍ
ءَامِنِينَ * لَا يَذُوقُونَ فِيهَا ٱلْمَوْتَ إِلَّا ٱلْمَوْتَةَ ٱلْأُولَىٰ
وَوَقَىٰهُمْ عَذَابَ ٱلْجَحِيمِ * فَضْلًا مِّن رَّبِّكَ ذَٰلِكَ هُوَ
ٱلْفَوْزُ ٱلْعَظِيمُ﴾

*But those mindful of God will be in a safe place amid Gardens and springs, clothed in silk and fine brocade, facing one another. So it will be. We shall pair them with maidens with beautiful eyes. Secure and contented, they will call for every kind of fruit. After the one death they will taste death no more. God will guard them from the torment of Hell, a bounty from your Lord. That is the supreme triumph.* [44:51-57]

## Fasting is a cleanse

The Muslim who seeks God's pleasure fasts continuously throughout the year. But we all await Ramadan with doubled enthusiasm, eager for its purifying qualities. Ramadan is a deep cleanse of the crust on the heart and a purification from sin. The Prophet ﷺ said, "*Whoever stands Ramadan in prayer, out of faith and hope for reward, will be forgiven his previous sins. And whoever fasts Ramadan, out of faith and hope for reward, will be forgiven his previous sins."*[1]

At the end of Ramadan, fasting becomes a familiar habit and a close friend. You continue on with its spirit, fasting the six white days of *shawwal*, the ten days of *dhul hijjah*, and the days of *Arafah* and *Ashura*.[2] You try to fast regularly on Mondays and Thursdays, as per the Sunnah, or even every other day. At the very least, you fast three days every month. Through this consistent practice of fasting, we are constantly purifying our sins. Take note that in his collection of hadith, Imam Muslim titled one of the chapters: *The Fast of the Prophet and How He Never let a Month Pass without Fasting.*

### FASTING IS SOLELY FOR GOD

The Prophet ﷺ conveyed that His Lord said, *"Fasting is for Me and I reward for it, for his desires and food are given up for My Sake. The fasting person experiences two joys: one when he breaks the fast, and another when he meets his Lord."*[3] This hadith should be enough incentive for the Muslim to observe regular fasts.

1 Al-Bukhari, *Sahih al-Bukhari:* Book of Fasting, #1901

2 *Shawwal* is the month following Ramadan, in which it is recommended to fast six days. *Dhul Hijjah* is the month in which Hajj falls, and the Day of *Arafah* is the most important day in Hajj (on which it is recommended for Muslims to fast if they are not performing the pilgrimage). *Ashura* is a day in the month of *Muharram* that commemorates Prophet Moses' crossing of the Red Sea, and on which the Prophet ﷺ encouraged Muslims to fast, along with the day before or after.

3 Al-Bukhari, *Sahih al-Bukhari*: Book of Fasting, #1904.

When we fast, we experience an earthly celebration of God's mercy, just by breaking our fast; it is a precursor to the heavenly celebration of joy and salvation from punishment in the next life. Abu Sa'eed Al-Khudri related that the Prophet ﷺ said, *"Whoever fasts a day for the sake of God, God will place a distance of 70 years between him and the Fire."*[1]

### The Ramadan prescription

There is a unique spiritual energy in Ramadan. The devils are chained, and the angels are dispatched, calling out, "Seeker of good, come forth! Seeker of evil, fall back!" Performing the obligatory acts of worship in Ramadan, like fasting and prayer, is the equivalent of seventy similar acts during other times of the year. The extra acts of worship in Ramadan are laden with as much reward as the obligatory.

Reward is ripe for the picking. It is the month of liberation from Hell, returning to God, seclusion in the mosques, and pursuing the Night of Power. Ramadan is a concentrated dose of spirituality that is unsurpassed by any other occasion or opportunity, except perhaps Hajj for the sake of God.

There are many ways to seek out the spiritual potential of Ramadan:

**The nights of Ramadan:** As the days of Ramadan are spiritual in nature because desires no longer hold the reins of the self, the nights of Ramadan are also blessed with a spiritual charge. Nights are spent in *tarāweeḥ*[2], a nightly habit

1 *Sahih Muslim*: The Book of Fasting, v. 1, #465; *Sunan Ibn Majah*, #638.

2 [**Translator's Note**]: Prayers performed in Ramadan after Isha.

of standing in prayer that should carry over for the rest of the year. The keenest worshippers will hasten to *tarāweeḥ* with diligence, making up any portions they may have missed each night. They will spend the hours before *suḥoor* (the pre-dawn meal) in prayer and supplication, calling upon God. They do not miss the morning meal, aiming to win the praise of angels and God Himself, Glory be to Him. The Prophet ﷺ said, *"Suḥoor is blessed. Do not abandon it, even if you only take a drink of water, for God and His angels praise those who eat suḥoor."*[1]

**Supplication:** Another spiritual benefit of fasting is the *du'ā*, a divine plea or supplication, that is always answered. The Prophet ﷺ said, *"The fasting person, upon the breaking of his fast, has a supplication that will not be turned away."*[2] The supplication at the moment of breaking our fast is an easy way to achieve happiness. It is a chance to plead for God to set our affairs aright and assign us to the highest levels of Paradise.

**The climax of the last ten days:** Muslims move from one good deed to the next in Ramadan, increasing their connection with God, and declining in their attachment to the world. As good deeds bring about new levels of faith, the soul craves being alone with its Lord. And so we turn to seclusion in the mosque in the last ten days, in order to strengthen our attachment to God. Our tongues recite the Quran day and night, and our hearing delights in it. Our minds are busy contemplating the magnificence of God's creation and the innumerable blessings upon his creatures,

1 *Sahih Muslim:* Book of Fasting, vol. 1 #466

2 Ibn Majah, *Sunan Ibn Majah: Book of Fasting*, # 1753.

until our eyes brim with tears out of fear of falling short and being subjected to God's anger and punishment.

The soul finds rest and peace in its hope in God's mercy, and so the nights are spent standing and sitting in front of the Lord of Existence, Glory to Him. The heart, body and soul are watered with contentment and new life. Through night prayers, *dua*, remembrance, seeking forgiveness, and shedding tears, we taste the sweetness of constant connection and being overcome with spirituality in the form of love, awe, fear and hope in God.

**Seclusion in the mosque.** *I'tikāf*[1] in the last ten days is a highly encouraged sunnah of the Prophet ﷺ. Aisha related that the Prophet ﷺ used to "tighten" his belt in the last ten days, bringing his nights to life and waking his family.[2] *I'tikāf* is an intense spiritual retreat in which we focus on polishing our souls and removing the accumulated crust of this world. It is not equivalent to a monastery, but is rather a short pause on the journey of life, during which we can take a good look at how far we have come and what is left of our journey. In this temporary solitude, we can hold ourselves accountable for how we have fallen short in the worship and service of God. *I'tikāf* is a short immersion in a sea of hope and fear, a journey to God with the provisions of mindfulness, and a quest to unearth the soul's potential.

1 [**Translator's Note**]: *I'tikāf* is a practice of staying in the mosque for a period of time to focus on worship and remove oneself from worldly affairs.

2 Al-Bukhari, *Sahih al-Bukhari:* The Benefits of Laylat Al-Qadr, #2024

Ramadan is a convergence of opportunities and worship practices that unleash the potential goodness and latent good deeds in the Muslim individual. It is filled with night prayers, reading Quran, constant remembrance, increasing the extra acts of worship, focusing on prayer, and deepening brotherhood and sisterhood in the mosques—all of this comes together with the powerful exercise of fasting for an entire month for a divine prescription of the highest strength.

Only the most unfortunate will miss out on all of this goodness, while only the mindful one will fully hit the target. For the most successful ones, their throats will be quenched at Ramadan's spring of love and worship. When the day of Eid comes, this individual stands to shake hands with the angels, dwelling amidst creation with true character, safeguarding the poor and weak, sensitive to people's needs, and forbearing of their mistakes. Thus is the soul shaped under God's watch, better prepared to bear the character and manners of Islam. After a month of seclusion and training, our human nature returns to its original state of purity. The soul shines brightly, and the heart is content.

## HAJJ

Hajj is a journey to God in which we as Muslims detach ourselves from all of the worldly concerns that have clung to us since birth, even our clothing. We break the habits that we have become accustomed to, such as wearing fragrances and oils, cutting our hair, clipping our nails, and covering our heads. During Hajj we leave our families and wealth behind, traveling to God stripped of everything but a genuine yearning for repentance, transformation, worship, supplication, and wholesome devotion. Each of these aspects of Hajj has various effects on one's spiritual life.

### Remembering the reward

Your heart is undoubtedly filled with pleasure when you know that a small deed carries a great reward. This is how someone performing Hajj should feel when they learn what God promises for anyone who sets off to His house for the purpose of Hajj or Umrah (a lesser pilgrimage to Mecca); it should bring immense comfort to them. Every Muslim on the face of the earth longs from the bottom of their hearts for God to bless them with the chance to make the Hajj pilgrimage to His house and visit His Prophet ﷺ. It is a fervent desire that the youth grow up with, adults toil for, and the elderly yearn for, all hoping to bring joy to their eyes and hearts with God's Holy House, Mecca, Mina, Arafah, Muzdalifah, and the blessed and illustrious city of Medina.

All of this stems from the countless references in the scripture about the virtue of Hajj and Umrah. For example, al-Bukhari and Muslim report with a chain from Abu Hurayrah (may God be pleased with him) that the Messenger of God ﷺ said: *"One Umrah to another is an expiation for what occurs between them, and an accepted Hajj has no reward but Paradise."*[1] Imam at-Tirmidhi, an-Nasa'i, and Ahmad also report with a chain to Abdullah bin Mas'ood that the Prophet ﷺ said: *"Perform Hajj and Umrah consecutively, for they extinguish poverty just like a blacksmith's bellows extinguish impurities from iron, gold and silver. An accepted Hajj has no reward but Paradise."*[2]

These textual references, as well as many others, generate a desire for Hajj in those who have been deprived of it. Anyone who has gone one or more times only increases in their affection and desire for repeating their Hajj or Umrah. You will not find any Muslim with a single shred of faith whose heart does not yearn for this spiritual journey—even the wicked sinners look forward to this ritual, with a genuine hope that God will bless them with it.

## Centering the heart's focus

Performing Hajj and Umrah is a golden opportunity to return your heart to purity and clarity, finding solace in remembering God. It is a journey of remembrance, quenching the heart with its ceaseless engagement. The body can be satisfied with a few small bites of food, but nothing quenches the heart like remembering God. When

1 *Sahih al-Bukhari*: The Book on Umrah, "The Obligation of Umrah," #1773; *Sahih Muslim*: The Book on Hajj, "The Virtues of Hajj and Umrah" v. 1, p. 566; Imam ar-Rabee' bin Ḥabeeb, *al-Jāmi' aṣ-Ṣaḥīḥ*, # 431

2 *Sunan at-Tirmidhi*, "The Reward of Hajj and Umrah," # 807; *Sunan an-Nasa'i*: The Book on Ritual Worship, "The Virtue of Consecutive Hajj and Umrah," v. 5, p. 115; This wording is collected by at-Tirmidhi, who called it a *ḥasan-ṣaḥīḥ* hadith.

you embark on Hajj or Umrah, leaving your worldly preoccupations for the blessed land of Mecca, you will feel like your heart was pulled through the clouds and tied to God's Great Throne as soon as you step foot in His Holy House—at that moment, the heart and tongue will know nothing but God's remembrance.

There are many indications in the Qur'an and Hadith that make clear that this is a journey of God's mention and remembrance in order to revive your heart. God, the Exalted, says:

﴿وَالْبُدْنَ جَعَلْنَاهَا لَكُم مِّن شَعَائِرِ اللَّهِ لَكُمْ فِيهَا خَيْرٌ ۖ فَاذْكُرُوا اسْمَ اللَّهِ عَلَيْهَا صَوَافَّ﴾

*And the camels and cattle We have appointed for you as among the symbols of Allah; for you therein is good. So mention the name of Allah upon them when lined up [for sacrifice]* [23:36]

He, the Exalted, also says:

﴿فَإِذَا أَفَضْتُم مِّنْ عَرَفَاتٍ فَاذْكُرُوا اللَّهَ عِندَ الْمَشْعَرِ الْحَرَامِ﴾

*But when you depart from 'Arafat, remember Allah at the sacred place [al- Mash'ar al-Haram].* [2:198]

He, the Exalted, also says:

﴿فَإِذَا قَضَيْتُم مَّنَاسِكَكُمْ فَاذْكُرُوا اللَّهَ

﴿كَذِكْرِكُمْ آبَاءَكُمْ أَوْ أَشَدَّ ذِكْرًا﴾

*And when you have completed your rites, remember Allah like your [previous] remembrance of your fathers or with much greater remembrance.* [2:200]

He, the Exalted, also says:

﴿وَاذْكُرُوا اللَّهَ فِي أَيَّامٍ مَّعْدُودَاتٍ ۚ فَمَن تَعَجَّلَ فِي يَوْمَيْنِ فَلَا إِثْمَ عَلَيْهِ وَمَن تَأَخَّرَ فَلَا إِثْمَ عَلَيْهِ لِمَنِ اتَّقَىٰ﴾

*And remember Allah during [specific] numbered days. Then whoever hastens [his departure] in two days—there is no sin upon him; and whoever delays [until the third]—there is no sin upon him—for him who fears Allah.* [2:203]

Additionally, ad-Dārimi reports that Aisha (may God be pleased with her) said: "The rituals of *ṭawāf* around the Kaaba, pelting the stones, and running between Mount Safa and Mount Marwa were only prescribed for God's remembrance."[1]

These excerpts from the scripture clearly demonstrate the importance of making your heart attentive with remembrance until it submits to God with serenity. You must undertake every ritual with this constant remembrance ingrained. Our

1 *Sunan ad-Dārimi*: The Book on Worship Rituals, # 1853; [**Translator's note:** These are rites of Hajj and Umrah. *Ṭawāf* is the circling of the Kaaba. Pelting the stones occurs in Mina and is exclusive to Hajj.]

mother Aishah may have mentioned only these iconic rituals, but intended God's remembrance to be upheld at all times; that is how souls strive and hearts heal.

## Chanting in universal harmony

The *talbiyah* is a ritual specific to Hajj and Umrah.[1] Ibn Majah reports with a chain from Sahl bin Sa'd that the Prophet ﷺ said: *"Whenever any Muslim chants the talbiyah, every single rock, tree, and clod of earth to his right and left until the end of the earth's boundaries chants the talbiyah as well."*[2]

The *talbiyah* chant represents responding to God's invitation out of not only fear and awe, but also love and longing. A person could not use the same terms used in this chant to respond to the call of their spouse unless they did so with intense love and the utmost delight—though any analogy made to God is deficient. When you chant the *talbiyah*, you announce that you are carrying a heart that loves God, hoping in His mercy and frightened by His punishment.

This *talbiyah* chant, however, is not limited to the one who makes it in response to God's invitation; it also stirs the love for God in the core of every creature around him. Every single rock, tree, speck of soil, and mountain on earth and in the sky bursts with the chant, reciting the beautiful words along with the one performing Hajj or Umrah. This is the greatest spectacle of attaining spiritual harmony with the universe, a harmony based on submission to God as Lord and an exclusive devotion to Him in worship.

1 [**Translator's Note:** This is the ritual of chanting "At your service, God, at your service!" throughout the duration of Hajj and Umrah.]

2 *Sunan Ibn Majah*: The Book on Hajj, "The *Talbiyah* Chant," v. 2 p. 974

This is a feeling that should energize your heart as you perform this rite, bowing to God in unison with all of these creatures. That is why God says alongside the verses about Hajj:

﴿أَلَمْ تَرَ أَنَّ اللَّهَ يَسْجُدُ لَهُ مَن فِي السَّمَاوَاتِ وَمَن فِي الْأَرْضِ وَالشَّمْسُ وَالْقَمَرُ وَالنُّجُومُ وَالْجِبَالُ وَالشَّجَرُ وَالدَّوَابُّ وَكَثِيرٌ مِّنَ النَّاسِ وَكَثِيرٌ حَقَّ عَلَيْهِ الْعَذَابُ﴾

*Do you not see that to Allah prostrates whoever is in the heavens and whoever is on the earth and the sun, the moon, the stars, the mountains, the trees, the moving creatures and many of the people? But upon many the punishment has been justified.* [22:18]

This ayah demonstrates the epitome of Muslims being in harmony with the world around them. This might explain why these rites take place in this blessed land; it hears God's remembrance, supplication, and the chanting of the *talbiyah* all year round, participating with the Hajj pilgrims in their chants. So these lands carry a spiritual vibe and an atmosphere of divine mercy that you will not find elsewhere. This is worlds apart from lands that suffer from all shades of wickedness and sin that take place therein. When the believers pass through the lands, their hearts ache, but they are soon relieved once they step foot within the boundaries of the lands of pilgrimage.

## POWERFUL PRAYERS

Supplication is the essence of worship and is an integral rite of Hajj and Umrah. Those performing Hajj and Umrah cry out in desperation to God with the utmost sincerity when they enter the state of *iḥrām,*[1] arrive at Mecca, and enter the Holy Mosque. They supplicate all throughout their circling of the Kaaba, as they drink Zamzam water, and while scurrying between Mounts Safa and Marwa. Then they continue to supplicate as they stand for hours at Arafah, when they make their sacrificial slaughter, and as they rest through the days and nights at Mina. The prophetic model is to supplicate at each of these stations, either with prayers that have been taught to us through scripture, or prayers that come straight from our hearts. The Prophet ﷺ used to pray to God during *ṭawāf*, specifically between the two final corners, by saying:

﴿رَبَّنَا آتِنَا فِي الدُّنْيَا حَسَنَةً وَفِي الْآخِرَةِ حَسَنَةً
وَقِنَا عَذَابَ النَّارِ﴾

*"Our Lord, give us in this world [that which is] good and in the Hereafter [that which is] good and protect us from the punishment of the Fire."* [2:201]

On Mount Safa, he would say in supplication: *"There is nothing worthy of worship but God, alone, without any partners. To Him belongs all authority and praise, and He is in control of all things"* (*lā ilāha illa Allāhu waḥdahu lā shareeka lahu, lahul-mulku walahul-ḥamdu wahuwa 'ala kulli shay'in qadeer*).[2]

1 [**Translator's Note:** This is the state of physical and spiritual purity that one declares to begin their pilgrimage.]

2 Malik bin Anas, *al-Muwaṭṭa'*: The Book on Hajj, "Beginning with Mount Safa in the Rite of *Sa'y*," v. 1, p. 532

The most intense stations of supplication where your prayers are most likely to be answered are as follows:

1. At the black stone: Al-Ḥākim reports with a chain from Ibn Umar (may God be pleased with him and his father): The Messenger of Allah ﷺ came to the black stone and touched it. Then he placed his lips on it, crying for a long while, and when he turned around Umar was crying too. He said: "Umar, here is where tears are shed."[1]
2. While drinking Zamzam water: Al-Ḥākim reports with a chain from Ibn Abbas that the Prophet ﷺ said: "Zamzam water is for whatever it is drunk for."[2]
3. On the Day of Arafah: This is one of the greatest days and times during which prayers are answered. Imam Malik reports with a chain from Talhah that the Messenger of Allah ﷺ said: "Satan is never seen to be more humiliated, outcasted, insignificant, and enraged than he is on the Day of Arafah. That is only due to Allah's mercy and tolerance he sees descending for the gravest sins."[3] Malik also reports that the Messenger of Allah ﷺ said: *"The greatest supplication is that on the Day of Arafah. The greatest thing that I and the*

1 This is narrated by al-Ḥākim in *al-Mustadrak* as well as in *aṣ-Ṣaḥīḥān*. He said: "This hadith has a *ṣaḥīḥ* chain" (ref. Numbers: 1670, 1/372).

2 *Sunan Ibn Majah*: The Book on Rites of Worship, "Drinking Zamzam Water # 3062 (from Jabir bin Abdullah); narrated from Ibn Abbas by al-Ḥākim, who said its chain was *ṣaḥīḥ*, The Book on Rites of Worship v. 1, p. 646, # 1739

3 Malik bin Anas, *al-Muwaṭṭa'*: The Book on Hajj v. 1, p. 422

*prophets before me said is: 'There is nothing worthy of worship but God"* (*lā ilāha ill'Allah*).[1]

These hadiths show us that we have a huge opportunity to increase our supplication, improve our repentance, and return to God by perfecting our requests of Him. We return after supplicating with our hearts softened by humility to God, but bolstered with hope in His divine mercy. Perhaps this—for those who experience it in truth—is of the greatest ways to attain the fulfillment at heart that God bestows upon anyone who comes to him in sincere supplication.

### Unwavering obedience

Performing Hajj awakens the most heightened senses of obedience to God without any hesitation in our hearts, sparking certainty that only God's commands will secure success in this life and the next and that God never intends evil for His servants. This blessed land reminds us of the story of the greatest act of obedience to God, that of our Prophet Abraham. He left his wife and child in this barren desert, void of any vegetation, livestock, food, or water. Then fresh pure water gushed forth from underneath the ground, nourishing the famished, quenching the thirsty, and healing all types of illness. When his son grew old enough to work alongside him, he was ordered to slaughter his child, the fruit of his loins, with his own hands. But he did not hesitate in his response, and his son was eager to comply with a command from God.

1 Ibid., v. 1, p.421

These locations came to serve as a symbol for this spirit of obedience. The yearly sacrificial slaughter became a tradition to remind everyone that the intellect is in need of revelation, and that the revelation cannot do without the intellect. It reminds us that the Muslim who complies with God's command without hesitation will achieve greatness in this life and the next.

### THE JOURNEY OF A LIFETIME

The Hajj rituals remind us of the afterlife. To this point, one scholar writes:

> Traveling to Hajj and Umrah is a reminder of your journey to the next life and the terrifying scenes of death. The vehicle you ride represents your ride in your coffin. Entering the desert and crossings its steppes to the demarcated boundaries reminds you of your exit from this world through death, arriving at your scheduled resurrection and witnessing the terrors of that day. Suffering through the separation from your family in the face of the dangers of the terrain and its predators represents your time alone in the grave, with nothing but maggots and snakes. Wrapping your *iḥrām* garment around yourself instead of your usual clothing is a reminder of your funeral shroud, as both of them are unsewn and wrapped around your body. Chanting the *talbiyah* in response to God's call represents your awakening response to the call on the Day of Resurrection when the trumpet is blown.

Then when you enter the sacred boundaries disheveled and dusty, it represents you rising from your grave, bewildered and stripped of clothing, gazing in awe alongside the crowd. When you then move on towards Mecca in droves of pilgrims, it signifies when people will walk towards Paradise, excited to enter. Finally, your entrance into the Holy Mosque to sit besides the Kaaba represents your audience with the Mighty Majestic King.[1]

1 al-Jeiṭali, *Qawā'id al-Islam*, commentary by Abdur-Rahman bin Umar v. 2, pp. 126-127

# Part II
# Character

Purification Prayer Zakah Fasting Hajj

# Purification

The ritual acts of purification have a significant impact on the character of a Muslim in many ways. One is that the requirement to constantly be physically purified of the substances that the Islamic code of conduct deems impure (all of which would normally disgust anyone with a sound nature and pure spiritual core) holds our sense of character to a high standard of hygiene. Physical impurities lead to the contamination of your character, which is why it is a pressing duty to purge these impurities from any garment, body parts, water, or location. This maintains cleanliness externally, allowing that purity to seep into our internal realities, and maintaining the natural disposition upon which God created our souls.

## Purification through speech

We find that the Prophet ﷺ taught us to use some powerful words for the act of removing and cleansing impurities. For example, the word for washing one's private part is *istinjā'*, which originally meant to rise or ascend, or to seek out a high place. The word *wuḍu'* comes from the word *ḍaw'*, meaning "illumination," and also *waḍā'ah*, meaning "something beautiful and clean." This is why Umar (may God be pleased with him) said upon seeing people he did not recognize kindling a fire, "O you people of the *ḍaw'!*"

meaning "glowing illumination," and didn't say: "O you people of the *nār!*" meaning "fire."

This goes to show how the Islamic tradition beautified everything, even the very words and terms we use. After all, God does command:

﴿وَقُل لِّعِبَادِى يَقُولُوا۟ ٱلَّتِى هِىَ أَحْسَنُ
إِنَّ ٱلشَّيْطَـٰنَ يَنزَغُ بَيْنَهُمْ﴾

*Tell My ⌜believing⌝ servants to say only what is best. Satan certainly seeks to sow discord among them.*
[17:53]

Whenever the Prophet ﷺ found out anyone named a child a revolting name, he changed it. Muslim narrates with a chain from Ibn Umar that the Prophet ﷺ saw a woman named *'Āṣiyah* (meaning "defiant"), so he changed her name to *Jameelah* (meaning "beautiful").[1]

## CONSIDERATION FOR OTHERS

A Muslim must grow accustomed to being pure so as to stay considerate of others. We must, for example, refrain from using the bathroom on roads and where people rest. Muslim reports that Abu Hurayrah narrates that the Prophet ﷺ said, *"Beware of the two things that cause one to be cursed."* They asked: "What are those two things, O Messenger of Allah?" He said, *"Relieving yourself on the people's road or in their area of shade."*[2]

1 *Al-Musnad*, v. 2, p. 18

2 *Sahih Muslim:* The Book on Purification, "The Prohibition of Reliving Oneself on the Road or in Areas of Shade"

This edict strengthens our consideration for preserving the environment around us and our mindfulness of not offending others.

### Conservation of God's blessings

One of the highly emphasized etiquettes of cleansing oneself, making *wuḍu'*, and bathing is to be conservative in our use of water, even if we were at a running stream. Ibn Majah reports that the Prophet ﷺ saw Sa'd using an excessive amount of water, and so he said, *"What is this wasteful extravagance, Sa'd?"* Sa'd asked: "Can one really be wasteful with water?" The Prophet ﷺ said, *"Yes—even if you were at a running stream."*[1]

This etiquette is not reserved only for ritual acts of purification, but also transfers over to the general approach of being moderate with all of God's blessings. This includes wealth, clothing, and eating and drinking. In a detailed description in Surah Al-Furqan, God lists the qualities of a distinctive group, "Servants of the Most Merciful." One of these characteristics is:

﴿وَٱلَّذِينَ إِذَآ أَنفَقُوا۟ لَمْ يُسْرِفُوا۟ وَلَمْ يَقْتُرُوا۟
وَكَانَ بَيْنَ ذَٰلِكَ قَوَامًا﴾

⌜*They are*⌝ *those who spend neither wastefully nor stingily, but moderately in between.* [25:67]

Were the nations that suffer from excessive use of fresh

[1] *Sunan Ibn Majah:* The Book on Purification, "Being Prudent when Making *Wuḍu'*," #425

water resources to use the rhetoric, laws, and etiquettes of Islam as a means of calling the people to use those water sources wisely, conservatively, and considerately, the people would comply promptly. This method would be highly effective and would save copious efforts to preserve these resources. It would ensure the sufficiency of these resources to improve the national agriculture, ridding struggling nations of a debilitating dependency on foreign supplies of basic food items.

### HABITUAL PURITY

Cleansing yourself of filthy substances and staying keen to wash yourself, make *wuḍu'*, and bathe every time the occasion calls for it (especially when attending public gatherings such as the Friday prayer and the two Eid prayers, entering Mecca, and standing at Arafah) keeps a Muslim neat and clean at all times. The prayers are spread all throughout the day and night, and when washing up for prayer after sleeping, the Prophet ﷺ even forbade us from dipping our hands into any vessel of water without rinsing it off first, for you do not know where your hand might have been during the night.[1] Then you make *wuḍu'* for the Fajr prayer, wherein your limbs that collect all types of dirt are washed. Later you make *wuḍu'* again for the sunnah prayers before noon, and during work you make *wuḍu'* again for the Dhuhr prayer. Upon returning from work, you wash away any remaining stains that may have caught onto you when

[1] Al-Bukhari, *Sahih al-Bukhari:* The Book on Purification, "Submerging a Potentially Dirty Hand into a Vessel is Disliked"

you make *wuḍu'* for the Asr prayer. Then for Maghrib and Isha, you eagerly continue this purification, staying free of filth and dirt all night.

This transforms purity into a habit ingrained into one's character, to the point that a Muslim would be indisposed to have any form of impurity touch him, even when it is not time for prayer. This is how we develop the highest standards of cleanliness: by putting them into practice as a form of worshipping God, in pursuit of His love and pleasure on the Day of Resurrection. It is even narrated about Uthman that he would pour water on himself every day out of worship to God.[1]

## Trustworthiness in Washing the Deceased

A person cannot forget these standards of manners and etiquette, especially when washing the deceased. It is not even allowed for anyone, righteous or otherwise, who cannot keep a secret to wash a dead body; the family of the deceased should choose someone with a heart that keeps secrets like a grave so as not to expose any confidential details about the departed.[2] If any bad signs in the body of the deceased are seen, such as a dark, gloomy looking face, then someone who cannot keep a secret would share what he saw with others, bringing sorrow to the loved ones and spiteful satisfaction to those who hated the deceased. This

1 Ibn Ḥajar, *Fatḥ al-Bāri*, v. 2, p. 421

2 Ibn Qudāmah, *al-Kāfi*, v. 1, p. 249; Ibn Qudāmah holds that trustworthiness is a condition in order to carry out the washing of a dead body, and that the one washing must not speak of any ill he sees.

is what Islam forbids, as Ibn Majah reports from Abdullah bin Umar that the Prophet ﷺ said, *"Let the trustworthy wash your dead."*[1]

## PRAYER

Prayer interacts with the character of the Muslim in many aspects. Our prayer keeps us sensitive to God's boundaries. God says:

﴿وَأَقِمِ ٱلصَّلَوٰةَ إِنَّ ٱلصَّلَوٰةَ تَنْهَىٰ عَنِ ٱلْفَحْشَآءِ وَٱلْمُنكَرِ﴾

*... and establish prayer. Indeed, ⌜genuine⌝ prayer should deter ⌜one⌝ from indecency and wickedness.* [29:45]

Prayer trains and refines our character. It makes us keen to maintain constant physical purity and cleanliness throughout the day and night. We stand up to have a dialogue with our Lord, leaving behind the vanities of this life to equip ourselves for the next. Then when we return to tending to this world, we employ our prayers to reach our goals in the next life as opposed to being completely immersed in the mud and muck of this life. We take advantage of what is good and wholesome in this life in order to energize us to continue to worship our Lord. We try to be careful not to revel excessively in this world's alluring facade, nor despair in distress when losing anything of it.

1 *Sunan Ibn Majah:* The Book on Funerals, "Washing the Deceased," #1461

## The habits of prayer

Prayer conditions us with good habits and expels our bad ones. It builds a habit of punctuality, as the ideal Muslim waits for the one prayer after the next and is keen to complete each prayer on time. And just as prayer builds the habit of doing things on time and not procrastinating, it also trains the soul to control its speech and movements for periods of time throughout the day. That is why al-Qurṭubi said:

Fasting controls desires, but prayer is a complete detention for the soul—and controlling a few desires is not like controlling them all. Though you curb your appetite for sex, food, and drink when you fast, you may still indulge in other types of desires such as speaking, walking, looking, and interacting with others. But in prayer you refrain from all of that, and so your limbs are restricted from your desires.[1]

The most common sins are those of the tongue. This is why the Prophet ﷺ said to Mu'adh, *"Is there anything that tosses people on their faces into the fire more than what they reap with their tongues?"*[2] Prayer trains us to control our speech by repeatedly demanding that we refrain from everything but the words of the prayer at fixed times throughout the day, until we acquire that beautiful character trait of only speaking good. To this point, Muslim narrates from Mu'awiyah bin al-Hakam as-Sullami:

> As I was praying with the Messenger of Allah

1 *al-Jāmi' li-Aḥkām al-Qur'ān*

2 *Sunan Ibn Majah*, The Book of Troubles and Turmoil, "Controlling Your Tongue during Turmoil"

> ﷺ, one of the men sneezed, so I replied, "May God show you mercy." Everyone shot looks at me, so I said, "May my mother lose me! Why are you all looking at me?!" They then struck their hands on their thighs... The Messenger of Allah ﷺ completed his prayer, and may my father and mother be sacrificed for him—I never saw any teacher before or after him teach more beautifully than he did. By God, he did not berate me, hit me, or insult me. He said, *"Casual speech is not fit for this prayer. It is only for glorification, exaltation, and the Qur'an's recitation."*[1]

## PRAYER BUILDS EMPATHY

Prayer forces us to take the feelings and human needs of others into account, and to bear in mind that they are, after all, human. The best way to handle these issues is to not deal with them roughly or harshly as long as the boundaries of God's laws are not crossed. For example, if you are hungry when the time for prayer arrives, then you should not force yourself to pray, suffering through the hunger and its unsettling pains. Rather Anas bin Malik narrates that the Prophet ﷺ said, *"When dinner is present, but the prayer has begun, begin with the dinner first."*[2]

1 Muslim, *Sahih Muslim:* The Book on Prayer, "The Prohibition of Speaking during Prayer"

2 Muslim, *Sahih Muslim:* The Book on Prayer, "Praying while Food is Ready is Disliked"

Likewise, during intense heat at the time of Dhuhr or the Friday Prayer, the Prophetic practice (*sunnah*) is to delay the prayer until the scorching heat subsides. This is seen in the narration of Abu Hurayrah (may God be pleased with him), wherein the Messenger of Allah ﷺ said, *"During intense heat, pray when it is cool, for the scorching heat is from the raging fire of Hell."*[1] Furthermore, the imam who leads the prayer should lighten the prayer as much as he can in order not to discourage people from praying. Al-Bukhari and Muslim both report a narration about this from Abu Mas'ood al-Ansari:

> A man came to the Messenger of Allah ﷺ and said, "I come late to the dawn prayer because of how this man lengthens the ['Isha] prayer." I had never seen the Prophet ﷺ become more angry in any admonition than he did on that day. He said, *"People! Some of you certainly scare others away! Any of you who leads the people must then make it brief, for standing behind him are the elderly, the weak, and those who have needs."*[2]

This is a major practical lesson in taking the feelings and circumstances of others into account so as not to cause difficulties for them. The Prophet ﷺ teaches us how to be

1 Muslim, *Sahih Muslim:* The Book on Prayer, "Delaying Dhuhr until it is Cool is Recommended during Intense Heat"

2 *Sahih al-Bukhari:* The Book on the Call to Prayer, "Complaining about the Imam when he Lengthens the Prayer," #704; *Sahih Muslim:* The Book on Prayer, "The Injunction for Imams to Lighten the Prayer"

empathetic even during prayer in the hadith narrated by Abu Qatadah: The Prophet ﷺ said, *"I sometimes stand in prayer wanting to lengthen it. But then I hear the crying of a child, so I make the prayer brief, not wanting to trouble his mother."*[1]

## PRAYER AND REFORM

Within the opening words of the prayer, we understand our role among the people. We are to be on the vanguard of society, working for reform, ideal citizens to be emulated, and role models to be followed. When the first generations of Muslim internalized these opening words for every prayer, they accepted for themselves nothing short of being witnesses over the people in place of the Prophet ﷺ. They came to the lands of Syria, Iraq, and Egypt, spread eastward to the Indian subcontinent, and spread westward to North Africa. The Muslims went on to conquer Constantinople and the lands of Eastern Europe, along with the region of Andalusia. The majority of the world was ruled by Muslims at one time, and God's promise to them came true. The words of the prayer impacted their hearts, improved their character, and changed the world.

## UNDERSTANDING AL-FATIHAH

Any Muslim who recites Surah al-Fatihah at least seventeen times each day would understand the importance of acknowledging favor and excellence—and the ultimate excellence belongs to God. In Surah al-Fatihah, we

1 al-Bukhari, *Sahih al-Bukhari:* The Book on the Call to Prayer, "Making the Prayer Brief when a Baby Cries"

acknowledge His favor upon us, and from this foundational understanding, we are grateful to anyone who has a right upon us or deals with us in excellence, for whoever does not thank the people does not thank God. Surah al-Fatihah helps us move on from being held captive by despair to the relief of having hope in God's infinite mercy, repeating the verse:

﴿ٱلرَّحْمَٰنِ ٱلرَّحِيمِ﴾

*the Most Compassionate, Most Merciful* [1:3]

Someone who recites Surah al-Fatihah so many times a day would always be working for the afterlife, never being neglectful of it, as it can either be the realm of true life and everlasting bliss, or the realm of a disgraceful punishment.

Reciting Surah al-Fatihah helps us stay determined to worship God, reliant on Him, and seeking His help, for all of this comes only with God's help. We distinguish ourselves from the path of the Jews and Christians, identifying with the prophets, the paragons of truth (*siddeeqeen*), the martyrs, and the righteous people whom God blessed. Surah al-Fatihah teaches us to treat others as they deserve to be treated—to be loving and compassionate toward the believers, and likewise toward others without any blind allegiance or injustice.

## Empowerment through humility

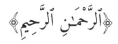

The Muslims who bow and prostrate to their Lord unconditionally refuse to direct these gestures towards anyone but God. This gives us dignity, for we refuse to bow before anyone or anything, fearing no harm from anyone but God. We are not made subservient by wealth, nor do we bow in front of even the most noble of human beings; we would never trade our religion for the world. We accept nothing for ourselves but an honorable and noble character, for when we bow down in prostration, we rise closer to the Most High and All Powerful God.

This empowerment causes us to perceive the most terrible tyrants and abominable oppressors as insignificant. This is why the Prophet ﷺ said, *"Whoever allows himself to be debased, willingly without being forced, is not one of us."* The great contemporary scholar Muhammad al-Ghazali writes:

Honor and dignity are of the most distinctive traits that Islam calls to and ingrains into society. It advocates for cultivating these traits through its theological doctrines and practices that it teaches. This was implied by Umar bin al-Khattab when he said, "I love to hear a man who is subjected to some form of humiliation say boldly: 'No!'"

Why is it that when the *muezzin* makes the call to prayer five times a day, he proclaims, "God is greater!" loudly at the beginning and the end of the call? And then these same words are repeated at every movement of the prayer itself? This is to instill in the Muslim a certainty, that never wanes or wavers, that any claimant to greatness after God is indeed small… It is as if this call to prayer was made to recalibrate the people after having been thrown off balance by the worldly life and led astray by its overwhelming distractions. To emphasize this point, God chose the two names *al-'Aẓeem* (The Greatest) and *al-'Aliy* (The Highest) as the names to be repeated when we bow and prostrate, so that our souls could wholly single out the Lord of all creation with greatness and high status.[1]

### A TRANQUIL REVERENCE

A Muslim learns to be still and reverent in prayer. If it is inappropriate for us to rush and recklessly speed through the streets in order to catch the prayer—compromising our dignity and reverence by doing so—then how could it be acceptable to do so for anything else! We are to face matters with calm souls and tranquil hearts, knowing that whatever comes our way never would have missed us, and whatever misses us never would have come our way.

We learn this practical lesson from the hadith narrated by Abu Hurayrah, wherein the Messenger of Allah ﷺ said, *"When you hear the prayer starting, then walk to the prayer. Be tranquil and reverent, and do not rush. Pray whatever you catch of the prayer, and complete whatever you miss."*[2] This hadith, along with others, outlines the path that a Muslim should follow, when going to pray or otherwise. The moral is to carry out whatever you catch, and complete whatever you miss.

### UPHOLDING RESPONSIBILITIES

On the other hand, prayer also teaches us to hasten in completing our duties as soon as possible, and to not procrastinate beyond the allotted time. If your conditions do not allow you to complete the prayer at the beginning of its time, you are not then exempted from completing it

1 *Khuluq al-Muslim*, pp. 205-206

2 al-Bukhari, *Sahih al-Bukhari:* The Book on the Call to Prayer, "Coming to Prayer with Tranquility and Reverence"

altogether. Missed prayers must still be made up at the first opportunity to do so. Muslim reports from Abu Hurayrah (may God be pleased with him) that when the Messenger of Allah ﷺ was returning of the Battle of Khaybar, they slept on the road one night, and he appointed Bilal to look out for the break of dawn. Bilal stayed up and prayed for a while, but then he was overtaken by sleep as he was leaning on his steed. The Messenger of Allah ﷺ did not wake up, and neither did Bilal or any of the other companions, until the sun hit them.

The Messenger of Allah ﷺ was the first of them to rise. He ﷺ became alarmed and said, *"Bilal?!"* Bilal said, "The same thing that overtook your soul overtook mine—and may my father and mother be sacrificed for you, Messenger of Allah!" He said, *"Follow me,"* and they followed him on their steeds for a bit. Then the Messenger of Allah ﷺ made *wuḍu'*, instructed Bilal to make the call to begin the prayer, and led them in the dawn prayer. When he completed the prayer, he said, *"Whoever forgets the prayer must then pray it when he remembers it, for God, the Exalted, says,*[1]

﴿وَأَقِمِ ٱلصَّلَوٰةَ لِذِكْرِىٓ﴾

*... and establish prayer for My remembrance.* [20:14]

This hadith makes clear how one should make up what he missed. Notice the alarm and urgency of the Prophet ﷺ and his companions when the time to complete their obligation had passed, and how the Prophet ﷺ left and moved away from

1 al-Bukhari, *Sahih al-Bukhari:* The Book on Mosques, "Making up Missed Prayers Promptly"

the place that caused them to miss the Fajr prayer because of Satan's presence there. He then made *wuḍu'* and prayed.

We learn from this that once an obligation becomes binding on you, you must complete it as soon as possible or at the first opportunity to do so. If ever you feel that there is a possibility that you will miss the opportunity for something important, you must rush to do it, so as to prevent any possible impediments. To this point, Muslim reports from Jabir bin Abdullah that the Messenger of Allah ﷺ said, *"Whoever fears that he will not arise before the end of the night should then pray the witr prayer at its beginning. Whoever hopes that he will arise before the end of the night, know that the prayer during the nights is witnessed, and that is better."* This is the right way for a Muslim to rush towards what is good and be keen to do it as soon as possible, not delaying an action unless delaying it is better for the action itself. If, however, one is doubtful in their abilities, then it is better to rush to do it during its time.

### A noble community

The prayer also helps in refining the *tarbiya* of a society. When a Muslim sees his brother in the mosque, he is free of any conceit, pride, or arrogance. When he or she attends the communal prayers, the study circles, and the gatherings of remembrance from a young age, they see that the Muslims are one rank, shaking hands with a deep-rooted love for one another, and praying for the good of one another. This coming together in prayer at the mosque is one of the most important foundations of *tarbiya* for the collective character of the community. It wards off negativity and individualism, and all of the societal ills that foster an irrational fear of others, spite for the community, and an aversion to interact and speak with fellow Muslims.

## ZAKAH

Zakah is to give a fixed percentage of wealth every year to those who need it. A love for wealth is naturally ingrained in our hearts; it can, however, become dearer to us than all else. Zakah is not only a source of benefit to the needy. Tempering the love for wealth through Zakah can shape and improve your character in so many ways.

### GREED IS A DISEASE

Zakah purifies the soul of the most severe moral and spiritual diseases. It is a cure for greed, as God says,

﴿وَمَن يُوقَ شُحَّ نَفْسِهِۦ فَأُو۟لَـٰٓئِكَ هُمُ ٱلْمُفْلِحُونَ﴾

*And whoever is saved from the selfishness of their own souls, it is they who are ⌜truly⌝ successful.* [64:16]

The root of this all-consuming disease of selfishness, which earns a person God's anger and the hatred of others, is cured by Zakah and charity. Giving Zakah and charity habituates us to give constantly, even when we don't want to, out of fear of God's punishment. We must continuously fight against our own self until it is subservient to us, and it is important to not withdraw and retreat from this internal battle when it is time to give in charity.

To help encourage us, there are 136 ayahs in the Qur'an that mention charity—either in general, or Zakah specifically. Thirty-three of those are direct commands to give, while the rest promote it and urge towards it.[1] This concept is so heavily emphasized in Islam in order to help us move away from the disease of avarice and on to giving with generosity and joy, hoping for the reward and protecting us from God's punishment that would have befallen us had we withheld.

### Spreading goodwill

Just as Zakah treats the disease of greed in the soul of the rich person who gives, it also treats the diseases of enmity and jealousy in the soul of the poor person who receives. This disease causes a person to look at the rich with scorn, envious that God gave to them but not to him. He is angry as to why society has not arranged for him to get a piece of the pie—why are *his* clothes tattered? Why is *his* mouth dry? Why is *his* child hungry?

Were these diseases of resentment to become widespread in any community, let alone a community of Muslims, it would lead to their destruction. These diseases fill a person's heart with a blazing fire that consumes him and tarnishes his character. But to share and show compassion to this person would engender within him a spirit of love, healing his heart and reviving optimism and hope. This generous sharing inspires him, when God improves his condition, to have no hesitation in sharing his own wealth, as when someone gave to him, it made him aspire to be the same

1 Salah al-Deen Sultan, *Sulṭah Waliy al-Amr fee Farḍ Waẓā'if Māliyyah*, pp. 180, 183

way. This peaceful form of cooperation is spoken about by Ali Izetbegović, the first President of Bosnia: "The goal of Islam is not to satisfy the rich, but rather to satisfy the poor."[1]

### BE THE HIGHER HAND

The rulings of Zakah teach us integrity and dignity. These concepts are shown in the hadith reported by Malik and al-Bukhari: Abu Hurayrah narrates that the Prophet ﷺ said, *"I swear by the One in whose hand is my soul, for any of you to take a rope and gather firewood on his back is better for him than to come to beg from another person, whether or not they give to him."*[2] Imam Ahmad reports that two men came to the Prophet ﷺ and asked him for charity. He looked up at them and saw them to be strong men, so he said, *"If you wish, I will give it to you, but this is not meant for the rich, nor the competent and able bodied."*[3]

These hadiths help us build a character of integrity that should turn us away from receiving Zakah, not coveting any public funds or private wealth. We are to exhaust all channels for permissible forms of work that would spare us the humiliation of begging. We must expend our efforts in order to benefit ourselves, giving charity so that our hands are the ones on top giving, not the lower ones asking for donations.

1 *Islam Between East and West,* p. 197

2 al-Bukhari, *Sahih al-Bukhari:* The Book on Zakah, "Refraining from Begging," #1470

3 ad-Dāruquṭni, *Sunan ad-Dāruquṭni:* The Book on Zakah, "Charity is not Permissible for the Rich," v. 2, p. 119; Ahmad; *al-Musnad,* v. 4, p. 224

### Growth through giving

Zakah teaches us to take on the qualities of generosity and selflessness, and teaches us what it means to share and sacrifice. Instead of averting our eyes and becoming agitated when we see the poor, out of fear that we would have to give them their due right and worry that our wealth would diminish, we become certain in God's promise to not only replace what we give, but also to increase it:

﴿وَمَآ أَنفَقْتُم مِّن شَيْءٍ فَهُوَ يُخْلِفُهُۥ وَهُوَ خَيْرُ ٱلرَّٰزِقِينَ﴾

*And whatever you spend in charity, He will compensate ⌜you⌝ for it. For He is the Best Provider.* [34:39]

This ayah should accelerate our generosity and sustain our habit of giving, invoking in us high expectations and a deep-rooted certainty that God will bless our wealth, exponentially exceeding what we give.

When you develop a habit of giving, God matches it. The Prophet's companion Abdul-Rahman bin 'Awf was a big philanthropist, and when he was asked about the reason he was so uniquely generous, he said: "God accustomed me with a habit, and I accustomed Him to a habit, so I will not break my habit with God causing Him to break His with me." He was alluding to the vast wealth that came from his incessant giving; if he were to stop giving, his wealth would stop growing.

### Cultivating a community of caring

Zakah lays a foundation of compassion and empathy within us. It cultivates a community practice of being acquainted with others and mindful of their circumstances. It builds a collective sense of assisting others in times of need and rushing to take care of them.

The Qur'an turns our attention to the important realization that some people may be in need of help, despite their inconspicuous appearance of not needing anything at all. God points out in describing some of the poor,

﴿يَحْسَبُهُمُ ٱلْجَاهِلُ أَغْنِيَآءَ مِنَ ٱلتَّعَفُّفِ تَعْرِفُهُم
بِسِيمَـٰهُمْ لَا يَسْـَٔلُونَ ٱلنَّاسَ إِلْحَافًا﴾

*Those unfamiliar with their situation will think they are not in need ⌜of charity⌝ because they do not beg.* [2:273]

Imam ash-Shafi'i said: "There are some people who can be rich off of one dirham so long as he is actively earning, and others who would still be in need with a thousand dirhams to his name because of his own inability and his many dependants."[1] This does not mean that we should investigate into people's private lives, but we should indeed be concerned about their needs so that we can help them before they are stricken by poverty or forced to ask.

## FASTING

Fasting is refinement for the character. It disciplines and trains the self to embrace higher behavioral standards. When we fast, we abstain from food, drink, and intimacy

1 Ibn Ḥajar, *Fatḥ al-Bāri*, v. 4, p. 307

from dawn until the setting of the sun, with a clear intention and the necessary soundness of body and mind. When we fast, we suppress the dominant desires that can drag us down into murky territory. Ibn Al-Qayyim, a 14th-century Islamic scholar and prominent spiritual thinker, said:

> Fasting is to restrain the self from desire, to wean from what has become too familiar, and to renew its capacity to resist temptation. With fasting, the self is primed to embrace what will lead to ultimate contentment in its eternal life and to accept what purifies it.

The sharp pangs of hunger and thirst are weakened over time while fasting, but when we feel them, we are reminded of the painful emptiness in the bellies of the hungry and poor. As the veins and intestines constrict with a decreased flow of food, so is satan constricted in his flow through the body and heart. The body naturally conserves energy while fasting, so the worshipper must save his or her energy for matters of the highest priority in this life and the next. The limbs are at rest, and desire is reined in.

Fasting is the bridle of those mindful of God. It is bliss for the spiritually developed and a workout for the pious. We learn to let go of what we enjoy in favor of obedience and love of God. It has a powerful effect of preserving the body and enhancing willpower. Fasting protects against the inevitable deterioration and pollution of life, which can be toxic if it becomes too concentrated in the self.[1]

1 Ibn Al-Qayyim, *Ẓād al-Maʿād*: v. 1, p. 211

### FASTING IS A BARRIER

Fasting builds a strong barricade between the Muslim and what Allah has made forbidden. When the Muslim is able to control himself by intentionally refraining from what is permissible, seeking help and reward from Allah while doing so, he is much better equipped to resist what is forbidden. A person indulges in forbidden actions because his desire is behind the wheel, and his willpower is too weak to protest. Fasting prevents this situation by restraining desire through a mandatory exercise in Ramadan, and through voluntary practice throughout the year. The Prophet ﷺ said about fasting, "*Whoever does not abandon lying in support of falsehood,*[1] *acting upon those lies, and acting ignorantly, Allah is in no need of his giving up food and drink.*"[2]

### FASTING REDUCES IMPULSIVENESS

The Prophet ﷺ taught us about the effects of fasting upon the character of the Muslim. He said, "*When you are fasting,*

1 [**Translator's note**]: *Qawl az-Zur,* lying in support of falsehood, is often translated as false testimony. However it is much broader and may take place within the scope of personal matters, disputes, and ethics, as well as media, political, and legal spheres. Sh. Muhammad Al-Ghazali writes in the book *Muslim Character,* "Lying in support of falsehood is a type of lie that is extremely dark. It is not just an attempt to hide the truth, but to eradicate it and place false information in its stead. It poses a danger to individuals in their personal affairs, and even more so to societies in their public affairs." (*Khuluq al-Muslim.* Dar al-Kuṭub al-Ḥadeethah, p. 39)

2 al-Bukhari, *Sahih al-Bukhari:* The Book of Fasting, #1903

*you should not be obscene or argumentative. If someone is rude to you, you should say, 'I am fasting.'*"[1] We cannot be impulsive while we fast; our tongue cannot run at will, and we should not raise our voice or speak rudely. Fasting trains the self to be more restrained and intentional, instead of driven by the desires of flesh, hunger and anger. When you have learned to control yourself, you have achieved one of the greatest accomplishments of character.

### Liberation from routine

Fasting frees a person from the usual constraints of routine and habit. We become so reliant on regular meals, comfort foods, late-night snacking, and caffeine breaks that we are convinced we cannot do without. Our moods and stamina are dictated by our stomachs. Then comes Ramadan to free us from those limiting habits, honoring our souls by breaking with menial routine. While fasting, we are no longer people who structure their day around the next meal. Our breakfast switches to the earliest hours of the dawn, and cravings are resisted until the evening. The Muslim ends the month freed from subservience to routine and the worship of anything except the Lord of Power—Glory to Him.

### Fasting heals selfishness

Selfishness is a chronic illness that can destroy a person. Within fasting lie the outlines of a cure for selfishness. Consider these hadiths and ponder their lessons: Jabir bin

1 *Sahih al-Bukhari:* The Book of Fasting, #1894; and also in *Al-Jāmi' aṣ-Ṣaheeh* by Imam ar-Rabee' bin Ḥabeeb, #330

Abdullah related that the Prophet ﷺ said, *"Beware of injustice, for it will be darkness upon darkness on the Day of Judgement. Beware of selfishness, for it destroyed those who came before you. It led them to shed blood and violate what was sacred."*[1]

Abu Hurayrah related that the Prophet ﷺ said, *"They shall not enter Paradise: the defrauder, the greedy, and the ungracious giver who holds his favors over people."*[2]

Ibn Abbas related that our Prophet ﷺ said, *"When Allah created the everlasting garden with His Hand, garnished its fruits and carved its rivers, He looked at it and said to it, 'Speak.' The garden said, 'The faithful have succeeded!' He then said, 'By My Power and My Majesty, the selfish shall not be near to Me in [the garden].'"*[3]

And the Prophet ﷺ said, *"The open-handed, generous one will be near to Allah, near to Heaven, near to people, and far from the Fire. The selfish and greedy one will be far from Allah, far from Heaven, far from people, and close to the Fire. A simple and generous person is more beloved to Allah than a selfish worshipper."*[4]

Fasting addresses the fault of selfishness through several methods:

**Generosity toward others:** The Muslim is encouraged to feed people upon the break of their fast, as in the hadith of the Prophet ﷺ related by Salman: "*When one feeds a fasting person, it is forgiveness for the sins and frees one's neck from the Fire. You share in the reward without decreasing at all from the faster's reward.*" The companions replied, "Messenger of Allah! Not all of us have enough to provide food for a fasting person."

1 *Sahih Muslim:* The Book of Piety, "Forbidding Injustice"

2 Ahmad

3 aṭ-Ṭabarāni

4 *Sunan at-Tirmidhi:* The Book of Piety," Generosity," #2027.

He ﷺ responded, *"Allah gives this reward for those who feed the fasting even if it is just with a single date, a drink of water, or a sip of milk."*[1]

Such a magnificent reward for just a small act of service is meant to ignite in the Muslim the desire to sacrifice and be open-handed. Give without hesitation, even when the amount is small or awkward. If unbridled generosity is a challenge, start by being generous with a small amount and gradually, step-by-step, the higher levels will be reached. The lightness and sheerness of our souls can draw us upward toward an untethered generosity.

**Fewer impediments to character development:** In the month of Ramadan, the doors of Hell are bolted, the doors of Heaven are flung open, and the devils are chained. A voice calls out, "Seeker of good, come forward! Seeker of evil, fall back!" These unseen forces support the Muslim in overcoming weaknesses in his character. It is the best time of the year to tackle selfishness and greed. We are able to work on increasing our generosity without the usual impediments.

**The example of the Prophet ﷺ:** The generous example of the Prophet ﷺ is another cure in healing our selfish natures. Ibn Abbas narrated that the Prophet ﷺ was the most generous of people in doing good, and he was the most generous of all in Ramadan, when he would meet the angel Gabriel to review the Qur'an. When Gabriel met with him, the Prophet was as generous as a free-flowing wind.[2]

1 *At-Targheeb wat-Tarheeb*, Al-Mundhiri, v. 2, p. 27; Reference was deemed *saḥīḥ* by Ibn Khuzaymah

2 *Sahih al-Bukhari*: Book of Fasting, "Generosity of the Prophet ﷺ in Ramadan," #1902

**Zakah al-Fitr:** The Zakah al-Fitr in Ramadan, an obligatory charity before the Eid prayer, is one of the most important acts of worship in Ramadan. It directly addresses greed and selfishness in the rich and poor, old and young, male and female. Even a newborn baby born in the hours before Eid prayer must be counted in the charity of al-Fitr by his or her guardian.[1] Thus, the entire community is enveloped in a spirit of giving and generosity.

Ibn Abbas related that the Prophet ﷺ said, "*Zakah Al-Fitr was prescribed as a purification for the fasting person from his idle talk and indecency, and it was prescribed to feed the poor. Whoever pays it before Eid prayer, it is the Zakah al-Fitr, and whoever pays it after the prayer, it is just a charity.*"[2] The Prophet ﷺ also said about Zakah al-Fitr: "*A sāʿ of dates or barley must be paid by every individual, young or old, free or enslaved, male or female, rich or poor.*[3] *As for the rich, Allah will purify their wealth, and as for the poor, Allah will return to them more than they gave.*"[4]

How amazing this is—the rich must give to the poor, and the poor must give to the poor. Everyone in the Muslim ummah, young, old and regardless of circumstance, must purify their wealth and give to the other in a divinely prescribed, collective generosity campaign.

1 *Sharḥ an-Nayl*, v. 3, pp. 289-294.

2 Ibn Majah

3 [**Translator's Note**: a *sāʿ* unit of volume used at the time of the Prophet ﷺ equivalent to a small container.]

4 Authenticated by Imam Ahmed, from *At-Targheeb wa At-Tarheeb* by Al-Mundhiri (2:100).

### Fasting tempers sexual desire

Fasting habituates Muslims to high levels of character and mindfulness, shielding them from impulsivity and disobedience. It is the recommended method for breaking the domination of desires over the self, particularly the sexual. Fasting prevents the Muslim from being driven by lust, stopping him or her from pursuing what is forbidden and destroying the lives and dignity of others. It keeps the Muslim from being consumed by sexual feelings through masturbation or other forbidden means, which can lead to overwhelming guilt and lack of willpower.[1]

The Prophet ﷺ said, *"Young men! Whoever among you can afford to should get married, for it helps in lowering the gaze and guarding chastity. If you cannot, then fast, for it will be a restraint."* Ibn Hajar explains this hadith further:

> Fasting essentially breaks desire. Excessive food and drink invite desires of all kinds to take control of the body, so fasting can be a restraint against the sexual impulse. This hadith can be understood as a prohibition of masturbation, since the Prophet ﷺ urged youth unable to marry to fast in order to curb their desire. If masturbation was permissible,

1 [**Translator's Note:** For Muslims who struggle to control unhealthy sexual behaviors, there are a number of community resources that can provide support and education, including the Family and Youth Institute (thefyi.org), PurifyYourGaze.com, and the directory of counselors by the Institute of Muslim Mental Health.]

> it would have been easier to refer to it in this context.[1]

If a man or woman engages in sexual activity while fasting, they have sinned and broken the fast. Even among married couples, desire is decreased by relieving spouses from sexual preoccupation during the fasting hours of the day, and even during the night for those who make i'tikāf (ritual seclusion in the mosques).

Whoever cannot resist sexual activity during the day in Ramadan must doubly compensate for that by fasting for two consecutive months. If that is not physically possible, he or she must feed sixty poor people as a penalty. All of this is a consequence for those who are unable to control themselves. This makes fasting one of the most powerful and practical methods for training in self-awareness, impulse control, and mindfulness of Allah.

### FASTING PURIFIES SPEECH

Another character development gained by fasting is the purification of the tongue. The Prophet ﷺ promised Paradise to those Muslims who control their tongues. The Prophet ﷺ also stated in an aforementioned hadith that whoever cannot avoid lying in support of falsehood, acting upon those lies, and ignorant actions, then Allah has no need of his fast.

Fasting, in truth, is the fasting of the body and tongue from everything that angers God. It is even recommended in *i'tikāf* that the worshipper minimizes his good speech.

[1] *Fatḥ āl-Bāri*, v. 9, pp. 2-14.

The tongue causes so many people to fall onto their faces into the Hellfire, and fasting teaches us to refine and control it. If we fast while allowing our tongues to backbite, argue, curse, and lie, then our fasts are meaningless and unsubstantial.

Anas bin Malik said that the Prophet ﷺ instructed some people to fast one day and told them, *"Do not break your fast until I give you permission."* So the people fasted until the sun set, but did not get permission to break their fast. A few of them went to the Prophet and said, "Messenger of Allah, I am still fasting until now so give me permission to break my fast," and he gave them permission one by one. But one man came and said, "Messenger of Allah, two young men are still fasting and they are shy to ask your permission, so please give them permission to break their fast." The Prophet ﷺ turned away. The man repeated his request, and the Prophet turned away again. Once more, the request was repeated, and the Prophet turned away.

Finally, Prophet Muhammad ﷺ spoke, *"They did not fast. How could they have fasted when they spent their day eating the flesh of people? Go and order them to vomit, if they are still fasting."* The man conveyed the words of the Prophet ﷺ and so the two youths threw up the contents of their stomachs. There was a large clot of blood in each container. The man told what happened to the Prophet ﷺ and he said, *"By the One in whose hand is my soul, if that flesh remained in their stomachs, they would have been consumed by the Fire."*[1] In another narration,

[1] Abu Dawud

the two youths vomited blood, pus, and rotten flesh until it filled the container. The Prophet ﷺ said, "*These are two who fasted from what Allah made permissible for them, then broke their fast with what Allah forbade them from. They sat by each other, and together they ate from people's flesh.*"[1]

A telling analogy for one who fasts while committing haram is a man who builds a palace while destroying the rest of the country, or one who refuses to take medicine but will readily gulp down poison.[2]

### FASTING INSTILLS MODESTY

Fasting nurtures one of the greatest character qualities in Islam: *Ḥayā'*. *Ḥayā'* encompasses meanings of modesty, shyness, humility, and decency, and can be translated in a character context as being ashamed to disobey Allah or engage in anything displeasing to Him. Zayd bin Talha heard the Prophet ﷺ say, "*Every religion has a hallmark, and the hallmark of Islam is ḥayā'.*"[3] Fasting is a special act of worship which none other than Allah can measure fully. A person could break his or her fast in private while pretending to fast in public, and no one would know. But a Muslim is shy to displease Allah and ashamed to disobey His command so brazenly. When *ḥayā'* becomes ingrained in a person, it brings forth only goodness.

### FASTING TEACHES TIME MANAGEMENT

Fasting teaches the Muslim to respect the value of time

1 *Musnad Imam Ahmad,* v. 2, p. 501
2 From Sa'eed Ḥawwa's *al-Mustakhlaṣ fee Tazkiyat an-Nafs*
3 Imam Malik bin Anas, *Al-Muwaṭṭa'*; Ibn Mājah, *as-Sunan*

and to use the hours in worship and obedience. If a Muslim intentionally eats just a few minutes after the *adhān* for Fajr prayer, or intentionally eats just a few minutes before sunset, a grave sin has been committed. A few moments can be the difference between an accepted fast and a null fast. Every minute is counted. The Muslim tracks his time in Ramadan with the highest accuracy; actions are not performed before their time nor delayed until after their time, just as employees must be disciplined and trustworthy in how they account for their work hours. This conscientious management of time is more than just a productivity tool, but also a central component of good character in the life of a Muslim.

## Hajj

Hajj is a major training ground for the soul. It conditions us to control our desires and temper our disobedience, and it is a source of unending good. All of the etiquettes, requirements, and recommendations of Hajj play a role in helping us build control over our own limbs, emotions, passions, and impulses.

We exercise self-restraint towards what is permissible in order to develop the strength to refrain from doubtful and sinful matters. Consider the restrictions of being in a state of *iḥrām*, which includes the prohibitions of: sexual intercourse and whatever may lead to it; idle, obscene, or sinful speech; arguing with others; wearing stitched garments, perfume, or dye; cutting any hair or nails; covering your head; attempting to hunt; and contracting marriages—all of these restrictions during the rites of Hajj help us restore our control over our behavior and actions. We are not allowed to release our eyes towards our spouses in a way that would give rise to lustful desires, or release our tongues with obscene words that would cause us to lose control with one another; our Hajj or Umrah would be invalidated, and we would be obliged to atone and pay the penalties for these actions. You are not even allowed to pull out the small hairs on your face or head!

These injunctions, as well as others, help bolster our determination, allowing the heart and mind to take the reins of our actions and emotions, as opposed to being controlled by our fleeting whims and hampering emotions. During the long days of Hajj, we go from being partially immersed—being only prohibited from intercourse—to being completely immersed in practicing a most beautiful patience. We build the habit of not giving in to the prodding of every passion and desire.

### DISCIPLINE THROUGH DETERRENCE

The rules of Hajj help us firmly control our limbs and feelings to be in compliance with what God and His Prophet ﷺ legislated. Anyone who violates any of the restrictions of the state of *iḥrām*, or of Hajj in general, incurs a monetary penalty. Such examples include:

1. Passing the *meeqāt* boundary without a state of *iḥrām* requires the sacrifice of an animal.[1]

[1] [**Translator's Note:** A *meeqāt* is a set location through which pilgrims must pass on their way to performing Hajj or Umrah.]

2. Someone who kisses his spouse without excretion of seminal fluid must sacrifice an animal, as does any form of non-penetrative intercourse without excretion. Penetrative intercourse invalidates the Hajj of both partners, and if it was consensual, then both partners must sacrifice an animal. If, however, the wife does not consent but is obliged against her will, then her Hajj is still invalid, but only the husband must sacrifice.
3. Whoever kills any hunting game, kills any animal in the sanctuary, or points someone else in a state of *iḥrām* to kill hunting game and then the latter does so, must sacrifice an animal.
4. Whoever plucks or cuts any hair must give charity for each hair. If it is over forty strands of hair, whether deliberately or accidentally, then he must fast three days, feed six poor people, or slaughter a sheep.
5. Whoever applies perfume to himself deliberately must wash it off, and must sacrifice an animal.
6. Whoever fails to pelt the stones or remain in Mina must then sacrifice an animal.
7. Whoever deliberately covers his head must sacrifice an animal.
8. Whoever wears any sewn garment or socks deliberately while sandals were available to him must take it off, and must also sacrifice an animal.

These penalties are highly effective in deterring those who cannot control their own limbs and behaviors without the fear of penalty. They will now abstain, knowing that they will have to pay a burdensome price for any action that is not within the boundaries of the rites and rituals. It is unthinkable that anyone would do any of those actions, even if they could easily afford to sacrifice an animal. Rather, we comply in order to come close to God and out of love for His religion. We hope thereby that our mistakes would be erased, and our sins would be forgiven. But there is no doubt that the human being needs effective preventative measures against violating Allah's limitations.

We can see how this holistic disciplining of where we look, what we say, and how we move, as well as controlling our passing thoughts and physical desires, leads to a purely refined character. These can be gateways to either the most noble character or the most crude. Through exercising strict control over those things from time to time, we can unlock the latent potential for good within them and unearth springs of righteousness in our behavior. Without this degree of control, you may end up like the many people who had high aspirations, but let the reins of their limbs and desires slip from their hands.

### A sacrifice of the self

Hajj shares its place among the other forms of worship in developing the traits of generosity and selflessness within us. We spend a large amount for Hajj, seeking God's pleasure, and would not hesitate to pay the price of any expiation for our negligence or violation of any of the requirements and restrictions of Hajj. We then make our sacrificial slaughter in order to feed the needy, our friends, and our travel mates. It is even recommended to bring extra provisions to Hajj in order to share them with your companions, building the habit of selflessness.

Professor Sa'eed Hawwa points out that one of the etiquettes during Hajj is to stock up on travel provisions and gladly share them with others, without being stingy or immoderate—though there is no such thing as being extravagant when giving. Ibn Umar (may God be pleased with him and his father) said: "A form of generosity is to share provisions during travel." It has also been said that a "blessed Hajj" is characterized by good speech and feeding others.[1]

## Sparing the burdens

Another quality that Hajj builds within us is to not covet nor be concerned with what others have, diverting the heart's gaze from what they eat, drink, and wear. Ibn Abbas reports that the people of Yemen came to perform Hajj, but did not bring any provisions with them, saying, "We rely only on Allah!" When they arrived in Mecca, they begged the people for help, and so God sent down the verse:

﴿وَتَزَوَّدُواْ فَإِنَّ خَيْرَ ٱلزَّادِ ٱلتَّقْوَىٰ﴾

*Take ⌜necessary⌝ provisions ⌜for the journey⌝—surely the best provision is righteousness.* [2:198]

'Atā' bin Abi Rabāḥ also reports that some would perform Hajj, making himself a burden for others. But then God forbade that.[2]

In line with this, it is prohibited to perform Hajj on a loan. Someone with good intentions might wish to fulfill their

1 Hawwa, *al-Mustakhliṣ fee Tazkiyat an-Nafs*, p. 66

2 An-Naysāboori, *Asbāb an-Nuzool*, p. 57

dream of performing Hajj or Umrah by taking out a loan to do so, but thereby subjecting themselves to humiliation by asking for money. This person will return from Hajj feeling humiliated all day and worried all night. We can now understand the high standard of character set by the hadith narrated by Abdullah bin Abu Awfa: "I asked the Prophet ﷺ if someone who has not performed Hajj yet should take out a loan to do so, and he said, *'No.'*"

### COMPASSION FOR YOUR COMPANY

Through Hajj, we learn to respect and take into account the feelings and circumstances of others. This explains a number of the rules of Hajj, including bathing before entering a state of *iḥrām*, entering Mecca, performing *ṭawāf*, and standing at 'Arafah—all of which are places of mass gatherings—so that we do not bother others with our body odor. We are also discouraged from crowding the black stone in a way that would risk the safety of others. 'Abdur-Razzāq reports in his *Muṣannaf* that the Prophet ﷺ said to Umar (may God be pleased with him), *"You are a strong man who can hurt the weak. When you perform ṭawāf around the Kaaba and see empty space around the black stone, then come close to it. Otherwise, say 'God is great,' and move on."*[1]

Furthermore, anyone who has an illness in their scalp or skin may cut their hair at any time. Ka'b bin 'Amrah narrates that the Messenger of Allah ﷺ saw him as lice was falling onto his face. He asked, *"Do those bugs bother you?"*

[1] 'Abdur-Razzāq, *al-Muṣannaf:* The Book on Hajj, "Crowding the Pillar, v. 5, p.36; al-Bayhaqi, *as-Sunan:* The Book on Hajj, "Touching the Black Stone when It Is Crowded," v. 5, p. 80

Ka'b replied, "Yes," and so he instructed him to shave his head while he was in al-Hudaybiyah.[1] Al-Qurṭubi said, "The scholars are in agreement that someone in a state of *iḥrām* may not shave, trim, or pluck his hair, except for someone with a disease."[2] Hajj also builds a sense of consideration for the feelings and conditions of others through the permissibility of riding during the rituals *ṭawāf* and *sa'y* (traversing the path between Mounts Safa and Marwa) for those who find difficulty in walking. Umm Salamah narrates, "I complained to the Prophet ﷺ that I was not feeling well, so he said: *'Perform ṭawāf after the people as you ride.'*"[3]

It is also permissible for the weak, women, children, and even men, to shorten their stay at Muzdalifah and pelt their stones before the break of dawn out of fear of the large crowd. Aishah narrates, "We stayed in Muzdalifah, and Sawdah asked the Prophet ﷺ for permission to leave before the stampede of people. She was a slow woman, so he let her."[4] Imam an-Nawawi said, "The Prophetic Way is for the person performing Hajj to stay in Muzdalifah until dawn. But it is recommended for the weak to leave before the dawn."[5] Ibn Ḥajar reports from 'Aṭā', who reports that Ibn

1 al-Bukhari, *Sahih al-Bukhari:* The Book on Hajj, #1814

2 *Tafseer al-Qurṭubi: al-Jāmi' li-Aḥkām al-Qur'ān,* v. 1, p. 758

3 al-Bukhari, *Sahih al-Bukhari:* The Book on Hajj, "Women Performing *Ṭawāf* alongside Men," #1619

4 al-Bukhari, *Sahih al-Bukhari:* The Book on Hajj, "Those who Leave at Night due to Weakness," #1681; *al-Lu'lu' wal-Marjān,* #812

5 an-Nawawi, *al-Majmoo',* v. 8, p. 105

Abbas told him that the Messenger of Allah ﷺ told Abbas on the night of Muzdalifah, *"Take our weak people and women. Let them pray the dawn prayer in Mina and pelt the stones at the last station before the crowd of people reaches them."* Ibn Hajar reports that 'Aṭā' would do this when he grew old and weak.[1]

Some rulings of Hajj even help preserve the wellbeing of tradesmen and businessmen by allowing them to engage with their properties. For example, it is reported that the Messenger of Allah ﷺ exempted the camel herders from spending the night outside of Mina, pelting the stones on the Day of Sacrifice, the two days afterwards, and on the day of departure.[2] The scholars used this analogy to allow anyone with property that would not receive the necessary attention to skip staying at Mina for the necessity of ensuring its wellbeing, which could not be otherwise maintained. Shaykh as-Sā'āti says in his commentary on *al-Musnad*, "To limit this exemption from staying at Mina to herdsmen would cause great difficulty, so it is extended to others as well." Imam ash-Shāfi'i also insists that anyone who is sick or has any property that they fear will go to waste, or anything that they fear they will miss out on, be allowed to leave as well.[3]

1 *Fatḥ al-Bāri,* v. 3, p. 528

2 Malik, *al-Muwaṭṭa':* The Book on Hajj, "Concession for Pelting the Stones," v. 1, p. 408; Abu Dawud, *as-Sunan:* The Book on the Rites of Hajj, "Pelting the Stones;" an-Nasa'i, "Pelting for Herdsmen"

3 See *al-Fatḥ ar-Rabbāni,* v. 12, pp. 223-224; aṣ-Ṣan'āni, *Subul as-Salām,* v. 2, p. 754; ash-Shawkāni, *Nayl al-Awṭār,* v. 5, p. 80; Ibn al-Qayyim, *Zād al-Ma'ād,* v. 2, p.290.

These rulings, which are amply supported by evidence, would help many Muslims today avoid stress and hardship in their Hajj experiences. People are usually overburdened by the overcrowding at the black stone during *ṭawāf* and at the pelting stations, where many have already died for this very reason. The rulings issued regarding pelting the stones in modern conditions, wherein over three million people are gathering for Hajj each year, must be revisited. It cannot be asked of all of these people to pelt their stones in just a seven hour window each day, as some rulings state.[1] We must attempt to protect these precious lives from being pushed to their limit of exhaustion, or even subjected to being trampled and dying under the soles of their own Muslim brothers and sisters. All of this occurs because of the insistence on following the letter, not the spirit, of our religion's beautiful law, a law that shifts its rulings from permissibility to prohibition when what is permissible leads to the destruction of lives. It might even be possible that someone who is weak, who knows that they would be trampled if they were to enter the dangerous crowd to pelt the stones, would be sinful for actually going through with it! Perhaps it would even be obligatory for him to pelt the stones at a later time during the night, or before noon, or to even save it for the next day. He may even appoint someone to pelt the stones on his behalf.

1 See: *Pelting the Stones and the Rulings Regarding It* by Dr. Sharaf bin Ali ash-Shareef, and *Rulings Regarding Hajj* by the esteemed group of scholars, Sh. Abdul-Azeez bin Baz, Saleh bin Uthaymeen, and Abdullah bin Jibreen. I suggest that this issue be revisited and requires an academic approach in order to save lives.

Hajj teaches us that this compassion is not limited to humans, but also extends to animals. The Prophet ﷺ taught us this through his commands regarding slaughtering a sacrificial animal during Hajj. Shaddad bin Aws reports that the Messenger of Allah ﷺ said, *"Allah prescribed excellence in everything. So when you kill, do so with excellence, and when you slaughter, do so with excellence. Sharpen your blade, and give relief to your slaughtered animal."*[1]

### UPHOLDING DIGNITY

The rulings of Hajj compel us to take on characteristics of nobility and honor. For example, Ibn Abbas narrates that the Prophet ﷺ passed by someone who had tied his hand to another person with a strap, a string, or something of the sort. The Prophet ﷺ cut it with his hands and said, *"Lead him by his hand."*[2] This hadith clearly demonstrates the extent of the Prophet's ﷺ awareness and sensitivity. Tying someone's hand and leading them with a rope is degrading to his humanity and diminishes his honor, and so he rushed to change this objectionable act with his own hands. He then provided a superior alternative, instructing him to lead him by his hand, not like an animal is led. This hadith represents a methodology of rejecting all forms of debasement to human dignity. Even the individual who commits a crime is punished not for the sake of humiliation, but with the goal of reforming his behavior and correcting his flaws.

1 ad-Dārimi, *as-Sunan:* The Book on Sacrificial Slaughter, "Excellence when Slaughtering," #1970

2 al-Bukhari, *Sahih al-Bukhari:* The Book on Hajj, "Speaking during *Ṭawāf*," #1620

### New limits

The long and taxing journey of Hajj, being forced to step outside of your comfort zone, and traveling by air, land, or sea is a form of torture. Abu Hurayrah reports that the Prophet ﷺ said: *"Traveling is a form of torture. It prevents you from your food, drink, and sleep. So when you complete your intended purpose, hurry back to your family."*[1]

The journey of Hajj restores your confidence in your own capabilities and the extent of your capacities. It reenergizes you to assume the responsibilities of Islam that rest on your shoulders, fulfill the trust, and testify to the truth among people and bearing witness. This journey of Hajj empowers us to excel in all of the facets of life that benefit us in the next life and the present one.

1 al-Bukhari, *Sahih al-Bukhari:* The Book on Hajj, "Traveling is a Form of Torture," #1804

# Part III
# The Mind

Purification Prayer Zakah Fasting Hajj

# Purification

Purification has clear effects on the development of the intellect. The mind is an integral part of an individual's state of ritual purity. It is unanimously agreed upon in the study of Islamic law that losing one's mind through temporary insanity, intoxication, fainting, or falling into a deep sleep all invalidate one's state of *wuḍu'*. When the intellect returns to its full function, you must renew your *wuḍu'* again. This is evidence of the connection between the mind and ritual purity.

## Purification teaches flexibility

The rules of purification trains within our minds a resilience and confidence that rejects rigidity. Limiting our consideration to only form and procedure would bring hardship to people, causing them to feel overburdened and imposing difficulty. In reality, the rules of ritual purification are characterized by ease and leniency. They call for the mind to be flexible and in tune with all circumstances, so as to be practical and applicable to real-life situations, without any undue burden.

One of the ways in which the intellect engages with ritual purification in a spirit of rational flexibility is the ruling regarding permissibility of using sea water. Travelers, merchants, laborers, and soldiers often have easy access to sea water. At the same time, it would be difficult for these types of people to carry around fresh water for purification, in addition to their drinking water. So the Prophet ﷺ facilitated their experience, as Abu Hurayrah narrates that he ﷺ said about sea water, *"Its water is pure, and the dead animals therein are permissible."*[1]

The practice of wiping over one's socks during *wuḍu'* also demonstrates the flexibility of purification rulings in Islam. Jareer bin Abdullah al-Bahili narrates, "I saw the Messenger of Allah ﷺ urinate, and then make *wuḍu'*, wiping over his socks."[2] Seventy of the Prophet's companions report the permissibility of wiping over the socks, and the majority of scholars hold that it is not an abrogated practice, as Ibn Rushd argued.[3] This practice is a major source of relief for Muslims, especially for those at work, those who are ill, physically weak, or constrained by time or space to wash their feet completely. Instead, they can wipe over their socks as long as they were in a state of purity when they put the socks on. The matter becomes even more flexible for a traveler, who can wipe over the same sock for three days, as opposed to the normal limitation of one day and night. This demonstrates the accommodation and receptivity within worship, an overarching spirit of practicality and

1 Malik, *al-Muwaṭṭa':* The Book on Purification, "Pure Water for *Wuḍu'*," v. 1, p. 22; *Sunan Abu Dawud,* The Book on Purification, "Making *Wuḍu'* with Sea Water"

2 Al-Bukhari, *Sahih al-Bukhari:* The Book on Wuḍu', "Wiping over the Socks;" Muslim, *Sahih Muslim:* The Book on Purification, "Wiping over the Socks"

3 Ibn Rushd, *Bidāyat al-Mujtahid waNihāyat al-Muqtaṣid*, v. 1, p. 18

ease, prompting the Muslim mind to always lean toward making things easy whenever difficulty is encountered, and as the difficulty increases, the room for facilitation does too.

Islam also does not obligate a woman who bleeds continuously outside of her period to bathe for every prayer, as that would cause great difficulty and excessive burden—it might even lead many women to stop praying altogether. Instead, a woman in such a predicament is only obliged to make *wuḍu'* before every prayer. She may continue to pray, even if her bleeding falls onto the carpet. This ruling can be found in the hadith of Fatima bint Qays.[1]

Perhaps one of the most impressively nuanced examples of providing ease in matters of purification is displayed in the following story of Ibn Abbas. Mujahid reports:

> We were in the mosque with Ibn Abbas as he was praying, when a man stood over us and asked, "Is there anyone who can give me a religious verdict?" We said, "Ask." He said, "Every time I urinate, a spurting fluid follows it." We asked, "The one from which children are born?" He responded, "Yes." We said, "You must bathe." The man then walked away, exclaiming, "*Innā lillāhi wa innā ilayhi rāji'oon!*"
>
> Ibn Abbas hurried through his prayer, and then said to 'Ikrimah, "Bring me to that man." Ibn 'Abbas came to him and asked him, "When

1 Muslim, *Sahih Muslim:* The Book on Menses, "Continual Bleeding"

> that happens to you, is there any feeling of lust within you?" He replied, "No." Ibn Abbas asked, "Do you feel any fatigue in your body afterwards?" He replied, "No." Ibn Abbas said: "This is just some dripping; making *wuḍu'* will suffice for you."[1]

When this man was given an invalid religious verdict that was not based on the principles of facilitation, it distressed him to the point that he exclaimed the phrase that we say when a calamity strikes us. Then when Ibn Abbas informed him of the legitimate Islamic verdict, the man rejoiced and was relieved of the stress caused by the first verdict.

A final example of rational flexibility in Islam's rituals of purification is the permissibility of making *tayammum* when water is not available. Imam Ahmad reports in his *Musnad* that the Prophet ﷺ said, *"Pure soil is a means of purification for the Muslim, even if he could not find water for ten years."*[2] But not only is *tayammum* permissible for someone who cannot find any water; someone who has access to water, but has a legitimate excuse to not use it may also make *tayammum*.

1 This narration shows us that true scholars issue verdicts to make things easy, while verdicts issued without proper knowledge complicate matters for people. It was common for the companions to only give verdicts for matters they knew about. They would occasionally direct a questioner to another companion, each doing so one after another, until the questioner ends up at the companion he asked first. This was out of their pious abstention to answer questions. For more examples, see *I'lām al-Mooqi'een 'an Rabb al-Ālameen* by Ibn al-Qayyim (v. 1, pp. 27-29).

2 Ahmad bin Hanbal, *al-Musnad*, v. 5, pp. 146-147

These excuses include anyone with an illness in which they would be harmed by contact with water, anyone who would be putting their wealth or property at risk by going to get the water, anyone who has a dire thirst and only enough water to drink, or someone who fears that the time for prayer would pass before they get to water. These examples show very clearly the extreme ease and leniency of Islam.

Aishah narrates that when she lost her necklace after the Battle of Banu Mustaliq, she held the Muslim army from moving on when they did not have any water. That is when the Quranic verse of *tayammum* came down. Usayd bin Hudayr said to Abu Bakr: "This is not the first display of your blessings, family of Bakr!"[1] The joy felt by Usayd bin Hudayr when the ayah of *tayammum* came down is the same joy that any Muslim who was ever forced into a circumstance in which they need to make *tayammum* feels. It is a powerful reminder of Islam's signature quality in promoting ease and relieving burdens in worship.

## Prayer

There are many ways in which prayer has an effect on the intellect. It is a divine, powerful, and far reaching way to shape the mind into maturity. This cultivation of the intellect is what the most brilliant have always strived for, as the pre-Islamic poet 'Antarah bin Shaddad writes:

1 Al-Bukhari, *Sahih al-Bukhari:* The Book on Tayammum, #334

*My horse obeys me with every stride*

*And I keep my mind sharp as I guide*

He praises his horse for being docile and quick, and his mind for setting the direction, as opposed to letting his whims guide him. The poet's moves are based on deep contemplation, and each decision he makes keeps his mind sharp; it is not filled with the foolish nonsense that everyone else's mind is filled with. Similar to this experience, prayer keeps our minds sharp and active, and it does so in a number of ways.

## Shaping the Muslim mindset

One of the pillars of the prayer (without which our prayer would be invalid) is to recite Surah al-Fatiha, and reciting another surah is recommended. The Prophet ﷺ would lengthen the Fajr prayer specifically, and the *tarāweeḥ* prayer in which the recitation of the entire Qur'an is completed during the month of Ramadan has become standard practice throughout the Muslim world. It is standard to recite for a long time during one's voluntary prayer in the middle of the night. The Prophet ﷺ once prayed two *rak'ahs*, reciting Surahs al-Baqarah, Ali 'Imran, and an-Nisa' in just the first *rak'ah*.

The practice of reciting the Quran shapes the intellectual foundation and mindset of Muslims. The incorporation of Quran in prayer develops a belief system based on facts and sources, rejecting speculation and guesswork. God says about those who follow speculative assumptions:

﴿إِن يَتَّبِعُونَ إِلَّا ٱلظَّنَّ وَإِنَّ ٱلظَّنَّ لَا يُغْنِى مِنَ ٱلْحَقِّ شَيْـًٔا﴾

*They follow nothing but ⌜inherited⌝ assumptions. And surely assumptions can in no way replace the truth.* [53:28]

The Muslim mindset is framed by sound belief, noble character, and comprehensive rulings. This intellectual framework has been shaped within the mind and conscience of every Muslim on earth, since the Qur'an came down and the companions taught it to the next generations. The Qur'an continues to echo within the minds and hearts of the believers throughout every place and time. As a result, there is a common mindset and an intellectual compatibility between all Muslims. Were you to conduct an experiment to compare the ideas of the citizens of a single country, asking them one hundred questions about various subjects such as the beliefs, behaviors, ideas, and laws in their region, the responses would vary greatly. But if you were to pose those same questions to a similar number of Muslims throughout different lands and ethnicities, their answers would be more compatible with each other.

This is because the Qur'an is the primary reference for every Muslim. It is the conclusive verdict and the ultimate wisdom from which all of our beliefs and ideas stem. The Qur'an defines for us the avenues which the mind should pursue, explore and expound, and the avenues that are beyond the grasp of the mind, in which we surrender to God. It employs our intellect in ways that are beneficial to us, sustaining it and keeping it fresh. The Qur'an does not let the intellect run wild, unrestrained by any guidelines or direction, exhausting its abilities in matters incomprehensible to the human mind, such as the nature of the soul. It is enough for us Muslims to read the verse:

﴿وَيَسْـَٔلُونَكَ عَنِ ٱلرُّوحِ قُلِ ٱلرُّوحُ مِنْ أَمْرِ رَبِّى وَمَآ أُوتِيتُم مِّنَ ٱلْعِلْمِ إِلَّا قَلِيلًا﴾

*They ask you ⌜O Prophet⌝ about the spirit. Say, "Its nature is known only to my Lord, and you ⌜O humanity⌝ have been given but little knowledge."* [17:85]

Despite the breakneck advancement of modern knowledge, scientists are still unable to reach any solid conclusions about the soul, the ultimate source of human life and activity. Without the soul, the body is merely a corpse, a vehicle which the Muslim and non-believer alike will bury beneath the ground one day. The Muslim understands the soul, heart, and body in light of the words of God and the Sunnah, using each in their proper framework and context.

Prayer maintains a basic framework of intellectual and spiritual beliefs, a mindset common to all Muslims. is what keeps the beliefs of every Muslim within reasonable boundaries. It gives our intellect direction, showing us the correct way to improve our condition in this life and the next. It flushes out our intellectual musings on what is of no benefit and what is futile for the human mind to pursue.

## PRAYER AND EXCELLENCE

Spiritual clarity certainly leads to an unsullied intellect and increased knowledge. As we mentioned before, prayer relieves stress and gives comfort to the heart, freeing the mind for contemplation, deep thinking, and mental sharpness. It gives us the chance to internalize what we learn, capturing the essence of God's words:

﴿وَاتَّقُوا اللَّهَ وَيُعَلِّمُكُمُ اللَّهُ﴾

*Be mindful of Allah, for Allah ⌜is the One Who⌝ teaches you.* [2:282]

Prayer has copious channels that flood us with *taqwa*, the mindfulness of Allah that leads to knowledge. When our communities are pure spiritually, scholars will then rise to distinction in every beneficial aspect of life, in medicine, astronomy, chemistry, optics, mathematics, and other fields.

### Prayer rulings highlight the status of knowledge

We cannot ignore the role of the religious laws regarding prayer in emphasizing the intellect, knowledge, and those who excel therein, as the one leading the prayer must be the one with the most knowledge of the Qur'an and Islamic law. Abu Mas'ood al-Ansari narrates that the Messenger of Allah ﷺ said: *"Let the one who is most well versed in God's scripture lead their people. If they are equally well versed, then let it be the one who is most knowledgeable of the Sunnah. If they are equally knowledgeable in the Sunnah, then let it be the one who emigrated first…."*[1]

Appointing the one who has mastery of the knowledge of

1 Muslim, *Sahih Muslim:* The Book on Mosques, "Who Should Lead"

the Qur'an and Sunnah as the leader of the prayer services is a clear indicator of the importance of knowledge in our religion. *"The most well versed,"* does not mean merely the one who memorized the most Qur'an, as the Messenger of Allah ﷺ appointed Abu Bakr to lead the prayer, while Zayd bin Thabit had memorized more than him—Abu Bakr even used to ask for Zayd's help in compiling the Qur'an. Ubay bin Ka'b was actually considered the one who knew the most Qur'an among the companions, as Anas narrates that the Messenger of Allah ﷺ said:

> *"The most compassionate person in my nation toward my nation is Abu Bakr. The one most firm in God's religion is Umar. The one with the most sincere form of modest reservation is Uthman. The most knowledgeable one in what is permissible and impermissible is Muadh. The one who is best versed in the Book of God (Mighty and Majestic) is Ubay. The one who is most knowledgeable in inheritance laws is Zayd bin Thabit. Every nation has a trustee, and the trustee of this nation is Abu Ubaydah bin al-Jarrah."*[1]

The abundance of mosques around the world reflects the abundance of those who have memorized and learned the Qur'an. Each community honors their knowledgeable members by electing them to lead their prayers, deferring

1 Ibn Majah, *Sunan Ibn Majah*, "The Virtues of the Prophet's Companions," #153; ash-Shawkāni, *Nayl al-Awṭār*, "Inheritance Laws," v. 6, p. 54; Ibn Hajar, *Fatḥ al-Bārī*, v. 2, p.21. The hadith is *ḥasan*, is reported by Ahmad, and was authenticated by at-Tirmidhi, Ibn Ḥibbān, and al-Ḥākim.

to their judgements in disputes, and seeking their guidance in times of trouble. This increases the respect of those with knowledge, encouraging them to further their learning even more in order to be worthy of the status that the people give them.

Rabee‘ bin Sulaymān al-Murādi was a student of Imam ash-Shafi‘i.[1] He used to give the call to prayer in the mosque where ash-Shafi‘i would teach his lessons on Islamic law and conduct gatherings of learning. He sat with the people to learn and excelled until he became the only one to transmit the first book on the science of Islamic Legal Theory (*Uṣul al-Fiqh*), *al-Risālah.* He and Imam al-Muzani became the main leaders for prayer, teaching, and issuing legal verdicts after Imam ash-Shāfi‘i. His position as the caller to the prayer did not prevent him from attaining this high esteem, because knowledge only raises one's status in the eyes of the Muslims.

1 His full name was ar-Rabee‘ bin Sulaymān bin Abdul-Jabbār al-Murādi. He was the caller to prayer in the mosque of Imam ash-Shafi‘i, and became one of his top students. He turned out to be a reliable scholar who taught classes in Egypt. Ash-Shafi‘i said about him, "There is no one I benefit more from than him." He also said: "I wish that I had spoon-fed him knowledge." He was the last to narrate reports from ash-Shafi‘i in Egypt, and both Abu Dawud and at-Tirmidhi reported from him. Al-Muzani would ask him for help with anything he may have missed from ash-Shafi‘i. Al-Buwayṭi said: "Ar-Rabee‘ is more trustworthy than me regarding ash-Shafi‘i." Al-Murādi was born in the year 147 H, and died in 270 H. For more, see *Tahdheeb at-Tahdheeb* by Ibn Hajar (3/254), and *Shadharāt adh-Dhahab* by Ibn al-‘Imād (2/159).

### Prayer rulings and the Fiqh of priorities

There are certain pillars to the prayer; if even one of them is missing, the prayer would be invalid. There are also certain actions that are recommended, *sunnah* actions, that increase your reward. This construct benefits the Muslim, training the mind to prioritize things properly. It teaches us to not give too much attention to the small things at the expense of more important matters, a mistake made by many who are immature in their religious knowledge. They see things as black and white, absolutely mandatory or prohibited, without any room in the middle for recommended or discouraged acts. These people, instead of treating people kindly, are a source of division and discord for their communities as a result of their misplaced priorities and lack of discernment.

The prayer, however, builds a clear framework in our minds that gives precedence to pillars and obligations over recommended actions when they cannot be performed together. Take as an example someone who has pain in their leg that prevents them from the recommended way of sitting in the stage of *tashahhud*,[1] but still insists on sitting in a manner that compromises their *khushoo'*. *Khushoo'* is the essence of focus and tranquility and the spirit of the prayer. This person is clearly wrong for doing so. A sound intellect would give priority to the spirit of the prayer over the non-obligatory forms. Another example of this is not praying a voluntary prayer if the obligatory prayer has started. Abu

1 **[Translator's Note]**: This is the position in prayer wherein one sits on their knees.

Hurayrah narrates that the Prophet ﷺ said: *"Once the prayer has been established, there is no prayer but the prescribed prayer."*[1]

We are currently in dire need to learn *fiqh al-awlawiyat,* the science of prioritization, both in personal and public life. We must learn and apply it to our *dawah,* our calling to Allah, and our collective Islamic movement, to our politics and economics. This can only happen if each of our minds are individually trained and developed to prioritize correctly the various matters in our lives.

### Prayer teaches intentionality

We learn through prayer to always have an objective for everything we do, to never do anything without a purpose, and to never be reckless in our decisions. Our prayers are only valid with the correct intentions. When we utter, *"Allahu akbar,"* to begin the prayer, our direction is made clear through the opening words: "I have directed my face towards the One who created the skies and the earth, whole-heartedly and submissively, and I am not one of the pagans." Then when you bow, you should remember what the Prophet ﷺ used to say in this position: *"God, I have bowed for you, believed in you, and submitted to you; my eyes and ears humbly submit to you"* (*Allāhumma laka rakaʿtu wabika āmantu walaka aslamtu; khashaʿa samʿee wabaṣari lillāhi rabb il-ʿālameen*). Then when you prostrate, you should remember his words to the same effect: *"My face has prostrated to the One who created it, fashioned it, and set therein its hearing and vision—blessed is God, the*

1 Muslim, *Sahih Muslim:* The Book on Mosques, "Starting a Voluntary Prayer after an Obligatory Prayer has Started"

*best of all creators!"* (*Sajada wajhee lilladhi khlaqahu waṣawwarahu washaqqa sam'ahu wabaṣarah—tabārak Allāhu aḥsanul khāliqeen*).

## LEARNING FROM THE CONCESSIONS IN PRAYER

When we are consistent in our prayers and maintain them regularly, we develop a mindset that is confident and versatile. We begin to learn about the various concessions that God granted us, allowing us to adapt to daily challenges with ease. It spares us from complicating matters and being too uptight and overzealous.

One example of this is the ease afforded to one who does not know the correct direction of prayer. When they try their hardest to figure it out, but still pray in the wrong direction, their prayer is still valid. This, however, is only if they truly exerted their efforts to figure it out.

Furthermore, someone who is physically incapable of standing may sit or lie down during prayer, or, if the handicap is severe, even gesture with their head or move their eyelids to signify the movements of prayer. What is important is that the prayer is not abandoned altogether.[1] Similarly, someone who does not have anything to cover the parts of their body that must be covered may pray while sitting down to ensure that their body is not exposed.

God has even permitted us to shorten our prayers when travelling and to combine the Dhuhr with the Asr, and the Maghrib prayer with the 'Isha—whether it be delaying one or praying the other one early. Aishah narrates, "The prayer used to be a mandatory of two *rak'as* in both travel

1 For more information, see *Fatḥ al-Bāri* by Ibn Ḥajar, v. 2, p.683.

and residence. The travel prayer stayed the same, but the prayer while resident was increased."[1] Abdullah bin Umar narrates that when the Prophet ﷺ would travel quickly, he would combine the Maghrib and Isha prayers.[2] Abdullah bin Abbas even narrates, "The Messenger of Allah ﷺ prayed the Dhuhr and Asr prayer together, as well as the Maghrib and Isha prayers, when he was not in a state of fear or travel" (Malik said that he holds that to have occurred during rain).[3]

Ibn Abbas applied this precedent once on a Friday when it was raining heavily; he instructed the caller to announce: "Pray in your homes!" Some criticized him, so he responded: "The one who is better than me did it. The Friday prayer is certainly obligatory, but I did not want to bring you out of your houses to walk through the mud and sludge."

## The impact of istikharah

The *istikhārah* prayer resolves any sense of reluctance from us. It makes us decisive and able to summon our mental and spiritual energies to achieve whatever objective God made our hearts inclined towards. It spares us any sense of hesitation. Whoever finds themselves in a predicament, unsure which direction to take, should resolve the indecision through prayer.

Jabir bin Abdullah al-Ansari reports: "The Prophet ﷺ used to teach us the *istikhārah* prayer just as he would teach us a surah from the Qur'an." The Prophet ﷺ said: *"When you*

1 Muslim, *Sahih Muslim:* The Book on Prayer, "Shortening the Prayer during Travel"

2 ibid., "The Permissibility of Combining Prayers during Travel"

3 Malik bin Anas, *al-Muwaṭṭa':* Shortening the Prayer during Travel, "Combining Two Prayers during Travel"

*decide on a matter, pray two rak'ahs of a voluntary prayer and then say:*

اللَّهُمَّ إِنِّي أَسْتَخِيرُكَ بِعِلْمِكَ، وَأَسْتَقْدِرُكَ بِقُدْرَتِكَ، وَأَسْأَلُكَ مِنْ فَضْلِكَ الْعَظِيمِ، فَإِنَّكَ تَقْدِرُ وَلاَ أَقْدِرُ، وَتَعْلَمُ وَلاَ أَعْلَمُ، وَأَنْتَ عَلَّامُ الْغُيُوبِ، اللَّهُمَّ إِنْ كُنْتَ تَعْلَمُ أَنَّ هَذَا الأَمْرَ خَيْرٌ لِي فِي دِينِي وَمَعَاشِي وَعَاقِبَةِ أَمْرِي - أَوْ قَالَ: عَاجِلِ أَمْرِي وَآجِلِهِ - فَاقْدُرْهُ لِي، وَيَسِّرْهُ لِي، ثُمَّ بَارِكْ لِي فِيهِ، وَإِنْ كُنْتَ تَعْلَمُ أَنَّ هَذَا الأَمْرَ شَرٌّ لِي فِي دِينِي وَمَعَاشِي وَعَاقِبَةِ أَمْرِي - أَوْ قَالَ فِي عَاجِلِ أَمْرِي وَآجِلِهِ - فَاصْرِفْهُ عَنِّي، وَاصْرِفْنِي عَنْهُ، وَاقْدُرْ لِي الخَيْرَ حَيْثُ كَانَ، ثُمَّ أَرْضِنِي بِهِ

> *God, I am seeking your help in choosing, based on your knowledge; I seek strength from your strength; and I ask You from your magnificent bounty. For surely You are all-capable, while I can do nothing; You are all-knowledgeable, while I know nothing; and you are most intricately acquainted with the unknown. God, if You know that this matter is good for me in my religion, my livelihood, and my fate in this life and the next, then make it possible it for me, easy for me, and bless me therein. And if You know that this matter is bad for me in my religion, my livelihood, and my fate in this life and the next, then keep it away from me and keep me away from it. Destine for me good wherever it may be, then make me pleased with it."*[1]

1 al-Bukhari, *Sahih al-Bukhari:* The Night Prayer, "Voluntary Prayers are Prayed in Units of Two," #1166; at-Tirmidhi, *Sunan at-Tirmidhi*, "The *Istikhārah* Prayer," #478

You should then weigh what your heart inclines towards, how much reassurance or apprehension lies in one direction or the other, even paying attention to your dreams for guidance. You can then move forward without any fear or apprehension about whatever you decided, because you laid your concern before your Lord, Mighty and High, and you can have confidence and trust in whatever Allah chose for you. This is how the *istikhārah* prayer cultivates in us the characteristics of confidence and strength. The great scholar Muhammad al-Ghazali said about it:

> It gives you an unwavering resolve and firm intention to pursue your goal through the proper means which bring you closer to Him. You exert all of your efforts in reaching your objectives, not leaving anything to chance or default, or letting fate determine anything you failed to prepare for yourself.

He continues on to rebuke those who lack these qualities:

> Islam hates for you to be irresolute in your decisions, confused about what is best and most judicious, and for there to be too many apprehensions in your mind. Doing this only creates for yourself an atmosphere of uncertainty and anxiety, and you will not know what to do. Your grip on that which benefits you becomes weakened, and those benefits slip away as missed opportunities. This confused, disoriented state is unbefitting of any Muslim.[1]

1 *Khuluq al-Muslim*, p. 65

## Overcoming doubt

Prayer helps us become accustomed to not feeling defeated by doubts, not being manipulated by satanic whispers, and not letting our certainty waiver because of doubt. For example, when you are uncertain about whether you passed gas during prayer or not, you should not preoccupy yourself with thinking about this for the rest of the prayer, succumbing to satan's distracting whispers. Instead we are instructed to stand firm in what is certain to us, as Abu Ḥurayrah reports that the Prophet ﷺ said: *"Whenever you feel something in your stomach, but are confused as to whether anything actually came out or not, then you must not leave the mosque until you hear a sound or smell an odor."*[1]

Similarly, when you are unsure about whether you have prayed three or four *rak'ahs,* you should stick to the lowest number about which you are certain rather than entertaining the distraction, pushing any doubt to the side. These distracting whispers and doubts are guaranteed to destroy even the strongest abilities of concentration, diverting you from what should be your prime focus.

From this prophetic methodology we learn how to deal with the lack of clarity and resolve from which some of us suffer. Such irresoluteness can lead down an ugly path, especially if one is in a position of responsibility and leadership—the people will begin to belittle his or her

1 Muslim, *Sahih Muslim:* The Book on Menstruation, "Continuing Your Assumption of Purity in Prayer when Any Invalidation of It is Doubtful," #99; at-Tirmidhi, The Book on Purification, "Making *Wuḍu'* after Flatulence," #75 (in a similar wording)

intelligence. When indecisiveness overruns a person's life, it can ruin a person's intellect, holding them back from realizing their full potential.

# Zakah

When we look at the practice of Zakah closely, we can see that it has many ways in which it shapes the mindset and intellectual foundation of the Muslim individual. Paying Zakah purifies the soul and cleanses the heart of its appetite for this world, freeing the mind to pursue knowledge. This is why the Prophet ﷺ said: *"There are two hungry people who will never be satisfied: the pursuer of knowledge, and the pursuer of the worldly life."*[1]

## Pursuit of wealth stagnates the mind

Someone whose heart is filled with the love of this world is always primarily concerned with more ways to accumulate and profit—it's all that is on his mind. Such a mind is not fit for knowledge. But whoever puts money in its proper place in their lives will maintain a balanced mindset, arranging their matters in this world and the next with proper emphasis and balance, practicing the words of Allah:

﴿وَيَسْـَٔلُونَكَ مَاذَا يُنفِقُونَ ۖ قُلِ ٱلْعَفْوَ ۗ كَذَٰلِكَ يُبَيِّنُ ٱللَّهُ
لَكُمُ ٱلْـَٔايَـٰتِ لَعَلَّكُمْ تَتَفَكَّرُونَ ۝ فِى ٱلدُّنْيَا وَٱلْـَٔاخِرَةِ﴾

[1] *The Compilation of the Rulings of Ibn Taymiyah,* v. 8, p. 28

> ... *They* ⌜*also*⌝ *ask you* ⌜*O Prophet*⌝ *what they should donate. Say, "Whatever you can spare." This is how Allah makes His revelations clear to you, so perhaps you may reflect - upon this world and the Hereafter...* [2:219-220]

Many people you meet today are investing all of their focus and mental efforts on increasing their material assets, or seeking a source of undiminishing wealth. If you try to start a conversation about something related to knowledge, show them a rare and valuable book, or share a powerful, wise insight, they become blank in the face, unable to respond with anything of substance. Instead of serving the Lord of all lands and skies, these people have become subservient to the land itself. They work like donkeys for a material future that may never come, but when you call them to the surety of reward in the next life, they respond with limp bodies and stale minds.

## INTELLECTUAL RIGOR IN THE LAWS OF ZAKAH

When we look into the books of Islamic Law at any of the debatable issues surrounding Zakah, such as whether one can pay the Zakah *al-fiṭr* in currency rather than in grains of food,[1] we find wonders of logic, intellect, and scholarly rigor. Upon learning these rulings, the Muslim mind is inundated with a wealth of perspectives, possible solutions, and comprehensive maxims. This scholarship is proof that within the detailed rulings of Islamic law lies a cultivation of

1 For more information, see *Taḥqeeq al-Āmāl fee Ikhrāj Zakāt al-Fiṭr bil-Māl* by Imam Ahmad bin Muhammad bin aṣ-Ṣiddeeq al-Ghimāri, 1989. It contains thirty-two different ways of proving the permissibility of paying Zakah *al-Fiṭr* with money.

intellect and thought. The nuances of our system of Islamic Law refines the intellect of someone who fully utilizes their mind to find the truth among the many opinions. Such a mind will be well-equipped to lead humanity towards improvement. The Muslim mind must be distinguished and unique. It must learn to explore, pioneer, and be creative in this world while keeping the next life as its ultimate objective. It must simultaneously consider the needs of soul and body, while balancing human brotherhood and social harmony.

## Fasting

The intellect is the frame of reference for the responsibility and entrustment of the human race. Mankind is distinguished among the creation by his intellectual capacity. Because of this intellect, human beings were appointed as trustees by God, a heavy responsibility that the skies, earth, and mountains refused to take on. Worship plays a vital role in the development and safeguarding of human intellect. In this chapter, we explore various ways in which fasting develops and stirs the mind.

### Taqwa leads to knowledge and wisdom

God says in the Qur'an:

﴿يَٰٓأَيُّهَا ٱلَّذِينَ ءَامَنُوا۟ كُتِبَ عَلَيْكُمُ ٱلصِّيَامُ كَمَا كُتِبَ
عَلَى ٱلَّذِينَ مِن قَبْلِكُمْ لَعَلَّكُمْ تَتَّقُونَ﴾

*You who believe, fasting is prescribed for you, as it was prescribed for those before you, so that you may be mindful of God.* [2:183]

If the goal of fasting is to attain *taqwa*, mindfulness of God, then know that this *taqwa* opens the door to wide vistas of knowledge and every kind of goodness.

﴿وَاتَّقُوا اللَّهَ ۖ وَيُعَلِّمُكُمُ اللَّهُ ۗ﴾

*Be mindful of God, and He will teach you.* [2:282]

*Taqwa* leads not only to knowledge, but to wisdom and all of the goodness associated with it. God says:

﴿يُؤْتِي الْحِكْمَةَ مَن يَشَاءُ ۚ وَمَن يُؤْتَ الْحِكْمَةَ فَقَدْ أُوتِيَ خَيْرًا كَثِيرًا ۗ وَمَا يَذَّكَّرُ إِلَّا أُولُو الْأَلْبَابِ﴾

*He gives wisdom to whomever He will. Whoever is given wisdom has truly been given much good, but only those with insight bear this in mind.* [2:269]

## Fasting invigorates the mind

When our stomachs are empty, our minds are more active and perceptive. As the saying goes, "Overeating diminishes intelligence." Mental sharpness is reduced when the stomach is full. Whoever eats too much and sleeps too much denies themselves much goodness. If we want to reach higher levels of knowledge and increase our intelligence, we should not be in the habit of filling our stomachs. When we are full, our bodies slacken, our senses dull, and we sleep longer.

Fasting in Ramadan, and throughout the year, decreases our food and drink intake and redirects energy to our brains instead of our digestive systems. This moderation in food keeps our minds sharp. It trains us in the skills of focused thinking and helps us stay up at night for the sake of knowledge.

### Qur'an develops the intellect

The increase in reading and listening to the Qur'an in Ramadan has a profound effect on our mind and frame of reference. The Qur'an consolidates the tools of knowledge in the minds of Muslims. It contains the foundations for empirical knowledge, for correct belief, and for the tenets of Islamic law. It provokes us to think deeply about the stories of earlier generations, those who obeyed and those who disobeyed. This process of engaging with the stories in the Qur'an is an important tool in intellectual development.

### Understanding wisdom behind rulings

Studying the rulings of fasting has an effect on the development and flexibility of the Muslim mind. There are numerous lessons that can be learned from the study of these rulings:

**Do not be carried away by enthusiasm.** The Muslim must look at situations logically, grounded in knowledge and an understanding of priorities. There is a saying that goes, "Restrain the impulse of emotion with the discipline of intellect." When young Abdullah bin 'Amr was so enthusiastic that he decided to commit to fasting every single day of the year, the Prophet ﷺ ordered him to fast less, with a maximum of every other day. He said, *"You don't know—you may live to an old age."* Abdullah later said, "I committed to the maximum that the Prophet ﷺ allowed, but when I grew older, I wish I had followed the Prophet's advice."

**Be reasonable and know your limitations.** The Prophet ﷺ forbade the practice of fasting continuously for two or more days without breaking fast at the proper time. He said, *"Beware of fasting continuously."* When the companions asked why the Prophet sometimes practiced continuous fasts himself, he answered, *"As for me, my Lord feeds me and gives me drink. Only take on deeds that you can handle."*[1] We should understand our abilities and limitations, and not take on more than we can physically handle. This requires a sound intelligence and insight. God says,

﴿لَا يُكَلِّفُ ٱللَّهُ نَفْسًا إِلَّا وُسْعَهَا ۚ﴾

*God does not burden any soul*
*with more than it can bear...* [2:286]

An intelligent flexibility is required in dealing with these situations in a way that achieves the goal without crippling stamina or health. A person's self-confidence can be shaken or destroyed when capability is misjudged. There may have been a few of the Prophet's companions who were at risk of committing to worship to the point of exceeding their capacity, for the Prophet ﷺ once commented, *"If this*

1 *Sahih al-Bukhari*: Book of Fasting, "The Punishment for those who Fast too Much"
*Sahih Muslim*: *Book of Fasting*, "The Impermissibility of Continuous Fasting, v. 1, p. 445

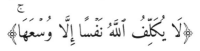

*month was lengthened for me, I would have fasted a continuous fast that would have taught a lesson to those who are overly zealous.”*

Our Prophet ﷺ wanted to teach his companions the valuable lesson of not exceeding limits. If it was a competition in endurance, the Prophet ﷺ could most certainly outperform them. He taught them to ground themselves in common sense and not overestimate their abilities and commitment in the long run. We should interact with the religion of God in the spirit of the ease for which it was designed, without excess and undue complication.

**Differences of opinion are part of Islamic life.** When we approach Islam with this flexibility and ease, we do not see ourselves as better than others. God alone knows who is truly mindful of Him, who practices *taqwa*. Abu Said Al-Khudri narrated, “We set out on an expedition with the Messenger of Allah, peace be upon him, on the 16th of Ramadan. Some of us fasted, and others did not fast. Those who were fasting did not hold it against those who were not, nor did those who were not fasting criticize those who were.”[1]

**Learn flexibility and be open to nuance.** The Muslim mind must be intellectually flexible in order to grasp the approach and wisdom behind rulings of fasting. For example, anything that enters the body that is impossible to prevent does not break the fast, such as the smell of smoke and perfume, or a small trace of water that may unintentionally reach the throat when carefully rinsing the mouth in *wuḍu’*. What enters the body through

1 *Sahih Muslim*: Book of Fasting, “The Permissibility of Fasting and Not Fasting for the Traveler in Ramadan,” v. 1, p. 453

the ear canal or the nasal passages, during sneezing or bathing for instance, does not invalidate the fast. Nor does a person break his fast with inadvertent semen leakage or vomiting. The fast of someone who accidentally eats or drinks, forgetting that he or she is fasting, is still valid. Eye drops and most injected medications do not break the fast. These nuanced rulings train our intellects to be flexible, introspective, and to look beyond the obvious.

# HAJJ

One of the clearest ways in which Hajj benefits the mind of the Muslim is in its relationship to our *taqwa*, or mindfulness of God. We can be certain that mindfulness of God leads to increasing our knowledge, as God says:

﴿وَٱتَّقُوا۟ ٱللَّهَ وَيُعَلِّمُكُمُ ٱللَّهُ﴾

*Be mindful of Allah, for Allah ⌐is the One Who¬ teaches you.* [2:282]

When we complete our Hajj with the correct requirements and etiquettes, then it will no doubt lead to being more mindful of God.

## WORSHIP AND MINDFULNESS

Completing the Hajj rituals, for example, must be performed with a sense of reverence for those rituals. They are the commandments of God and the tradition of His Messenger, and remembering this naturally increases our consciousness of God. God says:

﴿ذَٰلِكَ وَمَن يُعَظِّمْ شَعَـٰٓئِرَ ٱللَّهِ فَإِنَّهَا مِن تَقْوَى ٱلْقُلُوبِ﴾

*That is so. And whoever honours the symbols of Allah, it is certainly out of the piety of the heart.* [22:32]

God also points out that we do not come closer to Him through lifeless rituals that are void of any God-consciousness. That essence of God-consciousness is the prerequisite for any deed to be accepted, as God says:

﴿لَن يَنَالَ ٱللَّهَ لُحُومُهَا وَلَا دِمَآؤُهَا وَلَـٰكِن يَنَالُهُ ٱلتَّقْوَىٰ مِنكُمْ﴾

*Neither their meat nor blood reaches Allah. Rather, it is your piety that reaches Him.* [22:37]

He also says:

﴿إِنَّمَا يَتَقَبَّلُ ٱللَّهُ مِنَ ٱلْمُتَّقِينَ﴾

*Allah only accepts ⌜the offering⌝ of the sincerely devout.* [5:27]

Setting out for Hajj must be done with God-consciousness from the very start. God says:

﴿ٱلْحَجُّ أَشْهُرٌ مَّعْلُومَـٰتٌ فَمَن فَرَضَ فِيهِنَّ ٱلْحَجَّ فَلَا رَفَثَ وَلَا فُسُوقَ وَلَا جِدَالَ فِى ٱلْحَجِّ وَمَا تَفْعَلُوا۟ مِنْ خَيْرٍ يَعْلَمْهُ ٱللَّهُ وَتَزَوَّدُوا۟ فَإِنَّ خَيْرَ ٱلزَّادِ ٱلتَّقْوَىٰ وَٱتَّقُونِ يَـٰٓأُو۟لِى ٱلْأَلْبَـٰبِ﴾

*⌜Commitment to⌝ pilgrimage is made in appointed*

*months. Whoever commits to ⌜performing⌝ pilgrimage, let them stay away from intimate relations, foul language, and arguments during pilgrimage. Whatever good you do, Allah ⌜fully⌝ knows of it. Take ⌜necessary⌝ provisions ⌜for the journey⌝—surely the best provision is righteousness. And be mindful of Me, O people of reason!* [2:197]

Then towards the end, staying an extra day in the tents at Mina in order to pelt the stones must also be accompanied by mindfulness of God, as God says:

﴿وَٱذْكُرُوا۟ ٱللَّهَ فِىٓ أَيَّامٍ مَّعْدُودَٰتٍ فَمَن تَعَجَّلَ فِى
يَوْمَيْنِ فَلَآ إِثْمَ عَلَيْهِ وَمَن تَأَخَّرَ فَلَآ إِثْمَ عَلَيْهِ لِمَنِ ٱتَّقَىٰ
وَٱتَّقُوا۟ ٱللَّهَ وَٱعْلَمُوٓا۟ أَنَّكُمْ إِلَيْهِ تُحْشَرُونَ﴾

*And remember Allah during ⌜these⌝ appointed days. Whoever departs swiftly on the second day is not sinful, neither are those who stay behind ⌜till the third—seeking additional reward⌝, so long as they are mindful ⌜of their Lord⌝. And be mindful of Allah, and know that to Him you will ⌜all⌝ be gathered.* [2:203]

All of these evidences from scripture emphasize the strong link between Hajj and the mindfulness of God that we call *taqwa*. Such a state of mind subsequently leads to God flooding us with more and more knowledge.

## SUBMISSION OF THE INTELLECT

Some of the rulings of Hajj contain a display of the highest intellectual distinction that is afforded to the

Muslim, for whom contemplation is of the greatest means of increasing faith. Once our certainty is established and we submit whole-heartedly to God, we are able to carry out God's commandments, even when we are not able to understand that reason or wisdom behind the action itself. Such submission can be seen when Umar bin al-Khattab came to the Black Stone and kissed it. He said, "I know that you are just a stone—you neither harm nor benefit. Were it not that I saw the Prophet ﷺ kiss you, I would not do so." Umar is referring to the pure essence of our monotheistic creed, which asserts that only God can bring about benefit and harm; He is in full control of everything. Stones, on the other hand, have no power to do anything, and can bring no blessings to our lives. But kissing the Black Stone is done purely out of following the Messenger of Allah ﷺ, who says nothing of his own accord, but instead acted and conveyed God's unadulterated revelation to his people.

This attitude is of the distinguishing intellectual qualities of Islam. We as Muslims must find a balance between rationalizing the world around us with our minds, and submitting to the revelation at heart. Our multifaceted faith is composed of a fusion between applying reason to determine what will improve and enrich our lives, and deferring to God in matters to which we cannot determine any rhyme or reason—still, we must comply. These matters are from God, the Master of all creation, or are part of the revelation that God sent to His Messenger ﷺ, so we must avoid emphasizing only what we can rationalize at the expense of actions whose wisdom we cannot calculate.

## FACILITATION OF HAJJ RULINGS

The rulings of Hajj contain much leniency and flexibility, imprinting these important qualities onto the mind of the Muslim. We learn to always make things easy for people, and to avoid causing burden and difficulty for them. One example is how God permitted trade while in a state of *ihrām* during the days of Hajj. God knows that some of his servants will not be able to escape their albeit permissible business-savvy tendencies during the days of Hajj, and so He permitted that they engage in trade therein. Ibn Abbas narrates that the people used to conduct trade in Mina, Arafah, and the market of Dhul-Majāz at the beginning of Hajj, but then they feared to trade while they were in a state of *ihrām*. Then God revealed:

﴿لَيْسَ عَلَيْكُمْ جُنَاحٌ أَن تَبْتَغُوا۟ فَضْلًا مِّن رَّبِّكُمْ﴾

*There is no blame on you for seeking the bounty of your Lord ⌜during this journey⌝.* [2:198]

We see here the compatibility of our religious law with our natural tendencies. Our religion paints a picture of piety that does not unhealthily suppress our valid desires and romanticize monasticism. Our religion is the natural way, addressing our human passions and yearnings in a balanced way, preventing both indulgence and harshness.

This point is further emphasized by the other actions that are permitted while in a state of *ihrām*. Actions such as bathing, changing garments, and covering the head out of forgetfulness—a woman can even cover her face if she fears any sort of trouble that may arise. Those in a state of *iḥrām* are allowed to treat their wounds, scratch their heads and bodies, and even smell nice fragrances. In this state of ultimate piety and sanctity, we are even allowed to wrap a belt around our waists to keep our money, wear rings on our fingers, apply kohl, and take shade under awnings. All of these concessions demonstrate the flexibility of our religious law, which never overburdens any soul by depriving it of something that it needs, even in the state of *iḥrām*. The state of *iḥrām* is a state of abstention, but we only abstain to strengthen our will-power, not to torture ourselves, permitting for ourselves actions that we cannot do without.

The nature of ease in Hajj has been mentioned before with regards to minimizing the overcrowding at the pelting stations, allowing someone with a scalp disease to cut their hair early with certain parameters, and allowing the weak and ill to ride when making *ṭawāf* and leave the Muzdalifah camp early. We established that one must be considerate of others when pelting the stones, and that herdsmen and farmers (and by extension those who have other immediate concerns) may elect to spend time outside of Mina. All of this demonstrates the rational flexibility that a Muslim must learn to apply in order to create solutions, so as not to fall into the same stagnation that those with limited foresight and knowledge fall into. Their immature zeal leads them to make things complicated for themselves and others.

The order in which the rituals of Eid are performed also relieve us of burden and plays a role in building a foundation of flexibility in our mindset. Abdullah bin Umar narrates that the Messenger of Allah ﷺ stood up in front of the people in Mina as they were asking him questions. A man came and said to him, "Messenger of Allah, I was not aware, so I shaved my head before slaughtering." The Prophet ﷺ said: *"Slaughter; there is no problem."* Another man came and said: "Messenger of Allah, I was not aware, so I slaughtered before I pelted the stones." He said: *"Pelt the stones; there is no problem."* Ibn Umar continues to say that whenever the Messenger of Allah ﷺ was asked about an issue of doing one action before another, he said: *"Go on; there is no problem."*

All of these examples demonstrate the versatility of Islam, and its objective of facilitation and relieving burdens. This is how we should speak about Islam in our diverse contexts, representing it as God intended: without any undue burden that would drive people away from it. If Islam was presented in this way, people all around the world would flock to it in droves. I hold the Muslims themselves responsible, even more than non-Muslims, for the ugly picture of Islam that has been propagated and imprinted into the minds of the general public around the world.

## DIFFERENCES OF OPINION

The Islamic sources of law contains many indications of the leniency with which we are to engage with differing legal opinions. When Uthman led the prayer at Mina, he prayed it as four *rak'ahs*, as opposed to two, which was the practice of his predecessors. When this happened Abdullah bin Mas'ood said, "I prayed two *rak'ahs* (in Mina) with the Prophet ﷺ, and then two *rak'ahs* with Abu Bakr, and then two *rak'ahs* with Umar. Now your practices are starting to look different to me. How I wish I could pray two *rak'ahs*, still accepted by God, instead of four."[1] Ibn Hajar says in his commentary on this hadith, "He followed Uthman so as not to disobey, but he still made his opinion known."[2] We can take from this single incident both an intellectual and behavioral lesson on how to engage with a differing opinion. He followed Uthman, not out of a blind compliance, but knowing that he was simply leaving one valid practice (albeit more correct) for another, and each one has its respective proofs.

To show respect for someone else's opinion that is different from yours actually makes your mind more respectable in turn. This is the mark of a mind that is engaged in deep thought, weighing evidences against each other and engaging critically with what it learns. This is a mind that must be respected, even by those who most staunchly oppose its opinions.

## Debate should lead to action

The sources of our law also employ the mind to debate, but not merely for the sake of debating. The conclusions that are sought out are for either religious or worldly benefit, not to simply stock up on worthless knowledge. Abu Hurayrah narrates that the Prophet ﷺ said: *"God prescribed Hajj for you, so perform Hajj."* Someone then asked: "Every year, Messenger of Allah?" He said: *"Leave what I omit to me, for it was only the incessant questioning of and opposition to their prophets that killed those who came before you. If I prohibit you from something,*

1 al-Bukhari, *Sahih al-Bukhari:* The Book on Hajj, "Praying in Mina," #1657

2 *Fatḥ al-Bāri*, v. 3, p. 595

*then stay away from it, and if I instruct you with something, then do as much as you can of it."*[1]

Perhaps the Prophet ﷺ sensed that this question about the obligation of Hajj is typical of those who speak more than they act, who are quick to debate but slow to perform. So the Prophet ﷺ prohibited them from this. He teaches us to only look into that which will lead to action and from which we will benefit ourselves or those around us. We are to only ask about that which will improve this life or the next for us.

1 *al-Lu'lu' wal-Marjān:* The Book on Hajj, "The Obligation for Hajj is Once in a Lifetime," #846; I must clarify that this report starts with the statement, *"Leave what I omit for me..."* and all that came before it is taken from other narrations.

# Part IV
# The Body

Purification Prayer Zakah Fasting Hajj

# PURIFICATION

The body is the physical component and manifestation of the heart—which either beats with faith or is one of Satan's tools. Our minds are the source of our nature; the mind can be filled with truth and therefore display honorable character, or filled with doubts and display disgraceful character. Likewise, the energy and vigor of our bodies contain a latent potential for good that can either be activated to be counted among God's graceful servants, or kept buried under our desires to make us servants of Satan.

It is without doubt that the divine law in Islam emphasizes the needs of the body. Islam advocates for nourishing the body with that which will not be of detriment to its health, prescribing obligations and prohibitions to that end. A wholesome approach to strengthening the body while simultaneously avoiding the corruption of the soul and mind can only come from the One who created this complex human being. God says,

﴿أَلَا يَعْلَمُ مَنْ خَلَقَ وَهُوَ ٱللَّطِيفُ ٱلْخَبِيرُ﴾

*How could He not know His Own creation?*
*For He ⌜alone⌝ is the Most Subtle, All-Aware.* [67:14]

Modern civilization has taken unprecedented steps towards fulfilling the physical needs of the human being and providing all kinds of comfort, enhancement, and luxury, including in consumption, travel, and accommodation. From the comfort of your plush bed, you can turn the lights of your room on or off with the click of a button. Click another button and you can instantly be talking to another person on the other side of the world. With yet another click, you can instantly heat up water or food, start your car, and clean and dry your clothes. We think that we have more control through luxuries, but what we fail to realize is that by constantly satisfying our bodies, we are destroying our own abilities and strengths, making us fragile.

This outrageous overindulgence in feeding our bodies actually starves our souls from its due share of faith, and prevents our intellects from developing firm beliefs and character. We wake up in the morning concerned about our clothes, smartphone, and car, while contemplating which appetizing meal we want for breakfast. We dream of a bigger house and, especially when we're young, fantasize about a flawless spouse—then we realize that a picture-perfect marriage is actually a mirage. Our happiness vaporizes by the heat of our passions, and is overwhelmed by our incessant desire for more. People refuse to stop searching for bliss in this life, neglecting the permanent delight of the next. True happiness cannot be found in anything but Islam, submission to God, and in following its rules so that each facet of our existence can take its proper place in our lives.

We must live our lives with a balance of soul, character, mind, and body. Dr. Amin al-Khawli writes:

> The philosophy of Islam is not to defeat the

> body, nor to neglect or disgrace it, in pursuit of a purely spiritual life. Swearing off all worldly pleasures as monks do in order to disengage from this worldly life does harm to the body and fails to give it its natural due right. It is extreme and overzealous to the point of actually inflicting torture and suffering onto the body, causing a rupture in the natural harmony of the human existence. It accounts for the body at the expense of the soul.[1]

Islam is the divine balance that neither drowns the body in the mud of desires, nor deprives it from valid pleasures. In the following section, we will see how the various acts of worship are the highest forms of spiritual engagement, while simultaneously supplying the body with strength in many different ways.

There are many ways in which the rulings of purification in Islam lead to the betterment of the body. Imam al-Kāsāni defined purification as, "being cleansed of all types of physical and spiritual impurities."[2] The Maliki scholar Ibn Rushd writes that, "The Muslims are in unanimous agreement that the Islamic purification refers to two types: one from physical impurities, and another from spiritual impurities."[3] These linguistic and technical implications of the word "purification" surpass any term for hygiene in the modern world. Professor Muhammad Kāmil Abdul-Ṣamad writes:

1 *ar-Riyāḍah wal-Ḥaḍārah al-Islāmiyyah*, p. 55
2 *Badā'i' aṣ-Ṣanā'i'*, v. 1, p. 3
3 *Bidāyat al-Mujtahid wa-Nihāyat al-Muqtaṣid*, v. 1, p. 7

> A study of history will confirm that Islam was the first ideological institution known to man that promoted hygiene and worked against contamination. Islam was first to label something that was unsanitary or germ-infested as "filthy..." Islam determined thirteen things to be filthy, and they are what we know today to be sources of harmful bacteria. These include: pus, a copious amount of blood, feces, urine, vomit, a dog's saliva, a pig's flesh, and anything rotten, such as animal carcasses. Modern science will confirm that these are breeding grounds for bacteria... Islam established that if any of these catches onto someone's body, food, or drink, it would pose a risk of the presence of active harmful bacteria—and that is what it means to be "filthy" in religious terms, and "contaminated" in modern medical terminology. These matters are what is labeled in the Qur'an as "dirt" and the "filth of the devil."[1]

## A LINK BETWEEN PHYSICAL PURITY AND SPIRITUALITY

Islam demands physical purity while simultaneously promoting the spiritual, negating the various religious ideologies that insist that strength in the soul requires a neglect of the body. Some religions even have a concept called "holy filth," which is sought out by some monastic orders of

1 *al-I'jāz al-'Ilmi fil-Islām,* pp. 15-16; *aṭ-Ṭibb al-Waqā'i fil-Islām,* pp. 17-18

Christianity and Hinduism. The monks that shun physical cleanliness have deep spiritual feelings and claim that neglecting the body and deliberately ruining its cleanliness strengthens the spiritual component and sincerity of their prayers. They renounce any form of cleanliness and effort into maintaining their bodies, as mentioned by the prolific philosopher and first Bosnian president Alija Izetbegović in his book *Islam between East and West.*[1]

In contrast, Islam requires purity from all of these forms of filth with a remarkable emphasis. This physical purity is actually a means of attaining purity spiritually and cleansing our souls. We can see the inseparable bond between physical and spiritual purity when God says:

﴿إِنَّ ٱللَّهَ يُحِبُّ ٱلتَّوَّٰبِينَ وَيُحِبُّ ٱلْمُتَطَهِّرِينَ﴾

*Surely Allah loves those who always turn to Him in repentance and those who purify themselves.* [2:222]

The topic of purity is addressed thirty-one times in the Qur'an, integrating together the two concepts of physical and spiritual purification.

## Purification prevents against disease

The Islamic rulings of purification of the body draws our attention to all of the places that might be fertile grounds for the growth of germs, bacteria, and viruses. The practice of washing one's private parts (*istinjā'*), including the periodic shaving of the pubic region, is a clear example. Abu

1 *Islam between East and West,* p. 293

Hurayrah narrates that the Prophet ﷺ said: *"Five practices are part of the natural disposition: circumcision, shaving the pubic region, cutting the mustache, clipping the nails, and plucking under arms."*[1] Aishah also narrates: "Ten practices are part of the natural disposition: Cutting the mustache, letting the beard grow, brushing the teeth, rinsing the nose with water, cutting the nails, washing the knuckles, plucking the armpits, shaving the pubic region, conserving water..." (one of the narrators said: "I forgot the tenth, unless it was rinsing the mouth").[2]

We can see that washing the private parts and shaving the pubic region are means to remove any traces of urine or feces, and any germs that may have grown in the pubic hair. These are regions where filthy excrement combines with sweat, making it the most common area on our bodies where these germs that carry diseases can grow. It also prevents foul odors that would bother those around us, that we often find coming from those who do not cleanse themselves properly. Western practices—practices of the celebrities whom we idolize and imitate—that have crept

1 al-Bukhari, *Sahih al-Bukhari:* The Book on Seeking Permission to Enter a Home, "Circumcision in Adulthood and Plucking the Armpits, #6297; Muslim, *Sahih Muslim:* The Book on Purification, "Traits of the Natural Disposition;" Abu Dawud, *Sunan Abu Dawud:* The Book on Male Grooming, "Cutting the Mustache;" at-Tirmidhi, *Sunan at-Tirmidhi:* Manners, "Clipping the Nails;" Malik, *al-Muwaṭṭa':* The Description of the Prophet, "The Natural Disposition as Described in the Sunnah, v. 2, p. 921; Ahmad bin Hanbal, *al-Musnad*, v. 2, p. 229

2 Muslim, *Sahih Muslim:* The Book on Purification, "Traits of the Natural Disposition"

into the norms of Muslims, such as wiping oneself merely with napkins after defecating, eventually lead to an increase in bodily odor and contagious diseases. Water must be used to purify one's body, as God says:

﴿وَأَنزَلْنَا مِنَ ٱلسَّمَآءِ مَآءً طَهُورًا﴾

*We send down water from the sky as a means of purification* [25: 48]

In the case that water is unavailable, such as during travel or otherwise, then there are other ways to go about properly cleansing oneself after defecation. Using toilet paper might be warranted in this circumstance, but it should not be a regular practice to use it alone without water.

The Muslim obsession with cleanliness is one of the things that surprised Europeans when they came into contact with them. The Crusaders took great interest in these hygienic practices and brought them to Europe, despite the initial reactions of shock and disapproval of the general public. They were especially turned off by how many public bath houses there were in Muslim lands, where hot and cold water were readily available. Egypt alone had one hundred and seventy thousand public bath houses![1]

I once met a Muslim doctor based in Europe who was a specialist in female medicine. He complained that patients who apply all kinds of perfume and powders may still retain a repulsive odor on their bodies. I told him that this might be the case with some populations, but that Muslim women

1 'Izz al-Deen Farrāj, *al-Islām war-Ri'āyah aṣ-Ṣiḥiyyah al-Awwaliyyah*, p. 13

(and men alike) were obligated to wash themselves with water in order to protect themselves from developing the long-term body odors that would otherwise form.

Another Islamic practice that protects us from disease is the removal of armpit and pubic hairs. Pubic lice, or crabs, have infected human populations for thousands of years, and until today is considered an STD affecting a significant percentage of sexually active populations. These parasites have been linked to the spread of other contagious diseases. What's amazing is that this type of lice can be completely avoided by shaving the pubic region and armpits.[1]

Islam also demands that we clip our nails. It is one of the practices of the *fiṭrah*, the natural disposition, as mentioned by the hadith mentioned above. This is supposed to be an indicator of the Islamic character on one's appearance. It is well-known that there are diseases that spread through the hands by living on the nails. Germs collect under them that can carry diseases like typhoid, dysentery, and stomach viruses.[2] When Muslims make *wuḍu'* to pray five times a day, washing our hands as the first step and then with every step thereafter, and constantly keen to cut our nails, we are taking precautionary measures to protect ourselves from these diseases. It is perplexing that Muslim women sometimes allow their nails to grow, using nail polish that invalidates their state of *wuḍu'* and keeps them in a state of impurity. Every time they use the bathroom, the filth stays under their nails, whether or not they are aware of it. We

1 *Al-I'jāz al-'Ilmi fil-Islām,* p. 153

2 ibid.

should really reassess how deluded we are with following common beauty practices, permitting ourselves to adopt inferior characteristics in exchange for our noble tradition. Islam demands that every single fingernail be cut, not differentiating between the pinky and any other finger.

We are to pay very close attention to keeping our hands clean, to the point that we are strongly encouraged to never use our right hands to wash our private parts. Abu Qatadah narrates that the Prophet ﷺ said, *"None of you may touch your private part with your right hand as you urinate."*[1] In cleansing ourselves, we should use our left hand to clean and the right hand to pour the water if needed, as the right hand is the one we extend to people to shake their hands and to give them things. We also eat and drink with our right hands, so we should be careful not contaminate what we consume and the hands of others with our germs.

Another form of precaution that we as Muslims take is washing both hands after sleeping, before we make *wuḍu'*, and before and after each meal. Abu Hurayrah narrates that the Prophet ﷺ said, *"When you wake up from your sleep, wash your hand before you put it into the wuḍu' water, for you do not know where your hand has spent the night."*[2] You might have unknowingly touched your private parts as you were sleeping, and since you will use that same contaminated hand to touch and take things when you wake up, the

1 Muslim, *Sahih Muslim:* The Book on Purification, "The Prohibition against Washing the Private Part with the Right Hand"

2 al-Bukhari, *Sahih al-Bukhari:* The Book on Purification, "Not Dipping Your Potentially Contaminated Hand into the Water Receptacle"

Prophet ﷺ established the practice of cleansing it from any potential filth particles before using it to wash your mouth, face, or any other part of your body during *wuḍu'*.

Even in the very act of urinating or defecating, we are instructed to not do so on roads, shaded areas, still bodies of water, or under trees that bear fruit as Imam an-Nawawi points out.[1] Abu Hurayrah narrates that the Prophet ﷺ said, *"Beware of the two actions that invoke curses."* They asked, "What are they, Messenger of Allah?" He said, *"Relieving oneself on a road people use, or in their shaded areas."*[2] Jabir bin Abdullah also narrates that the Prophet ﷺ prohibited urinating in still-standing water.[3] These scriptural examples certainly provide a Muslim with a heightened consideration to not harm others, but additionally protect us from being harmed by any diseases that people might catch if they come into contact with these filthy substances. The fecal matter of someone who is infected with ancylostoma carries this disease to others. The ancylostoma, known as hookworms, are equipped with sharp teeth that will tear away at the membranes of the intestines, causing sores,

1 *al-Majmoo'*, v. 1, p. 87

2 Muslim, *Sahih Muslim:* The Book on Purification, "The Prohibition of Relieving Oneself in Roads and Shaded Areas"

3 ibid., "The Prohibition of Urinating in Still Water;" Imam ar-Rabee', *al-Jāmi' aṣ-Ṣaḥīḥ*, #163; Shaykh as-Sālimi debated with Ibn Ḥazm about his position on permitting urination in water that is running, as the objective is to not contaminate (*Ma'ārij al-Āmāl*, v. 3, pp. 98-101)

bleeding, and iron deficiency.[1] Urinating in still-water leads to schistosomiasis, which is proven to spread and put others at risk through urination in water. If we look at the resources spent to cure those infected by schistosomiasis, also known as bilharzia, and the damage the disease does on the liver, we see that it has taken a large chunk of the budget of some developing nations. Following the prophetic guidance would have not only protected the individuals, but also saved these societies from diseases that have destroyed both their public health and their national budgets.

Knowing that every cubic inch of the earth carries millions of microbes, we see that the limbs most commonly exposed to these germs are the hands, the mouth, the nose, the face, and the feet. These, not coincidentally, are the limbs that we wash during *wuḍu'*, cleansing them of these microbes that may have caught onto them, especially in environments filled with dust, smoke, and widespread pollution. Just think about how prevalent violations are to the policies of environmental protection agencies around the world, causing harmful effects to humans, animals, and plants alike. The limbs that we wash in *wuḍu'* are the limbs that have the most exposure to this pollution. We as Muslims, then, are constantly limiting our exposure to these contaminations through our mindful efforts to clean ourselves for the five daily prayers. Professor Muhammad Kāmil 'Abduṣ-Ṣamad writes:

> Modern science confirms that making *wuḍu'*

1 'Izz al-Deen Farrāj, *al-Islām war-Ri'āyah aṣ-Ṣiḥiyyah al-Awwaliyyah*, p. 61

> reduces the occurrence of cancerous tumors that are caused by chemical substances. *Wuḍu'* makes sure to remove them before these substances build up to an amount that would enter the body through the skin, leading to cancer… This is shown by the fact that skin cancer is most prevalent in western societies, such as the United States and Australia, despite the sun's rays not being as strong in those areas as they are in others. *Wuḍu'* keeps the skin moist and reduces the sun's harmful effects on the skin. The practices of *wuḍu'* and bathing also remove sweat that contains salt and other particles. If the sweat were left to dry, it would stay on the skin and block the sweat glands.[1]

Regularly rinsing your mouth and brushing your teeth, which the Prophet ﷺ himself did with the *siwāk*, a natural toothbrush, has a profound effect on keeping the mouth, gums, and teeth in good shape; it even prevents bad breath. When we study the books of Islamic Law, we see that most scholars hold rinsing the mouth to be a recommended act of *wuḍu'*,[2] but the scholars of the Hanbali *madhhab* even hold that rinsing the mouth and nose is a pillar of *wuḍu'* without which one's *wuḍu'* is invalid.[3] We should also consider the

1 *Al-I'jāz al-'Ilmi fil-Islām*, pp. 21-22; *aṭ-Ṭibb al-Waqā'i fil-Islām*, p. 20

2 Ash-Shafi'i, *Kitāb al-Umm*, v. 1, pp. 33-34; about brushing the teeth with the *siwāk*, he says, "It is recommended at all times."

3 Ibn Qudāmah, *al-Kāfi*, v. 1, p. 26; al-Buhooti, *Kashf al-Qanā'*, v. 1, p. 96

hadith wherein the Messenger of Allah ﷺ said, *"Using the siwāk purifies the mouth and pleases the Lord."*[1] The Prophet ﷺ also said, *"Were it not that I would be burdening my nation, I would command them to use the siwāk at every prayer."*[2]

Modern medicine only increases our certainty as Muslims that every ruling in our religion is of benefit to our bodies, minds, souls, and hearts; every ruling benefits us in both this life and the next. Rinsing the mouth cleanses our gums and between our teeth of the cavity-forming bacteria that can cause great pain and complications in the teeth, in addition to the fact that it keeps our mouths looking and smelling pleasant. Rinsing your mouth regularly in this way keeps your mouth constantly free of any residue that would cause bad breath or hurt your teeth.

It has been scientifically proven that the *siwāk* contains many substances that play an essential role in maintaining dental hygiene.[3] Fluoride, for example, mixes with one of the components on the enamel of the tooth called hydroxyapatite to create fluorapatite, which in turn strengthens the enamel against the acidity that is secreted by cavity-causing bacteria. It also decreases the acidity of the bacteria inside the mouth, decreasing the risk of tooth

1 *al-Musnad,* v. 6, p. 47

2 al-Bukhari, *Sahih al-Bukhari:* The Book on the Friday Prayer, "Using the *Siwāk* on Friday;" Muslim, *Sahih Muslim:* The Book on Fasting, "Using the *Siwāk*"

3 For more information, see *aṭ-Ṭibb al-Wiqā'i fil-Islām,* Dr. Ahmad Shawqi al-Fanjari pp. 33-34; *al-Islām wat-Tarbiyah aṣ-Ṣiḥḥiyyah,* Dr. 'Aida al-Banna 33; *al-I'jāz al-'Ilmi fil-Islām*, Muhammad Kamil Abdul-Samad 119-121.

erosion. The *siwāk* also stunts the growth of cavity-causing bacteria when its bristles are used to massage the gums, reactivating the blood circulation.

Silicone removes the remnants of food and discoloration in the enamel of the tooth. The alkaline in the *siwak* moistens the mouth and freshens the breath. It stops the activity of bacteria in the mouth, and even protects against infections in the gums and tissue surrounding the tooth. The tannin substances and waxy components of the *siwāk* strengthen the mucous membrane of the gums and surrounding tissue. The wax components also encase the tooth with an extra protective layer against cavities.

Many medical studies have been done about the effect of the *siwāk* on dental hygiene. One study performed in Ghana involved 887 participants: 450 men, and the rest women. The study found that 83.7% of the participants did not suffer from loss of teeth and had very low rates of cavities. In 1981, a study was done in Pakistan, which found through practical examination that using the *siwāk* decreased the risk of blood cancer. A national institute for health research in America performed a study on the components found in the *siwāḳ*. The study concluded that using the *siwāk* prevents some cancerous diseases, and that those who the *siwāk* are less likely to develop cancerous diseases.

Washing the nose with water (known in Arabic as *istinshāq* or *istinthār*) does not only involve washing the outer part of the nose with water, but also rinsing the inside of the nostrils with some of the water too. This allows the water to reach the small hairs inside the nose. Blowing the water out of the nostrils powerfully three times cleanses the nose of any particles that may have entered it through the air. The nose is the main passageway used for breathing, so if one does not constantly keep it clean, it will stay contaminated by any dust or microbes that get caught in its inner hairs. The inner nose hairs lose their ability to purify the air that we breathe by being filled with these contaminants, allowing the polluted air to enter our lungs and cause diseases like meningitis. It can also cause infections in the inner ear and nostrils.

Ear, nose, and throat doctors are aware of all of this, and thus recommend constantly rinsing the nose so that bacteria and microbes do not collect and accumulate inside of the nose, ruining our main way to breathe. Some even recommend placing a piece of cloth over the nose, but rinsing your nose five times a day is easier and a more simple solution. Some professors from the Medical University of Alexandria performed a study on hundreds of residents in their city for two whole years. They took a sample from each of their noses and examined them. They found that the nostrils of those who did not pray (and thus did not make *wuḍu'*) were pale, oily, and affected by the dust particles that entered it. The openings of their nostrils were sticky and dark, and the hairs had fallen out. The smaller hairs inside of the nose were stuck together and covered with dust particles. Those who prayed and made *wuḍu'*, on the other hand had nostrils that were clean and free of any dust particles, and their hairs were free of anything harmful.[1] Such hygiene in the nose prevents diseases like influenza, polio, and diphtheria, as Dr. al-Fanjawi mentions.[2]

1 *al-I'jāz al-'Ilmi fil-Islām,* Muhammad Kamil Abdul-Samad, p. 19

2 *aṭ-Ṭibb al-Wiqā'i fil-Islām*, p.24

## ABSTAINING FROM INTERCOURSE DURING MENSTRUATION

The Qur'an speaks about the blood of menstruation in the most elegant way. God says:

﴿وَيَسْـَٔلُونَكَ عَنِ ٱلْمَحِيضِ قُلْ هُوَ أَذًى فَٱعْتَزِلُوا۟
ٱلنِّسَآءَ فِى ٱلْمَحِيضِ وَلَا تَقْرَبُوهُنَّ حَتَّىٰ يَطْهُرْنَ﴾

*They ask you ⌜O Prophet⌝ about menstruation. Say, "Menstruation is a painful condition, so keep away, and do not have intercourse with your wives during their monthly cycles until they are purified.* [2:222]

It is important to note that in Islam, menstruation signifies only a physical impurity, and has no implications on spiritual purity. Some civilizations used to shun menstruating women completely, and perhaps other religions took this idea from them. Islam takes a different, practical approach; menstruation is a physical impurity, and intercourse is forbidden during its duration. Women must bathe after the period ends and wipe the area with a perfumed cloth.

It has been proven that intercourse during menstruation leads to disease, as Dr. Adil Raslan mentions in his research *al-'Alāqah al-Jinsiyyah Ghayru Sawiyyah wa Amrāḍuha* (Abnormal Sexual Relations and their Diseases), presented at the International Islamic Medical Conference in Cairo, 1987.[1] Doctors list many complications and risks to both the man and woman due to having sexual relations during menstruation. God relieved Muslim women and men of this

1 Conference Journal, p. 5

harm by mandating abstention from intercourse during the course of a woman's period.

### THE IMPURITY OF PORK

The impurity of the meat and lard of pigs is agreed upon, as God says:

﴿قُل لَّآ أَجِدُ فِي مَآ أُوحِيَ إِلَيَّ مُحَرَّمًا عَلَىٰ طَاعِمٖ
يَطۡعَمُهُۥٓ إِلَّآ أَن يَكُونَ مَيۡتَةً أَوۡ دَمٗا مَّسۡفُوحًا أَوۡ لَحۡمَ
خِنزِيرٖ فَإِنَّهُۥ رِجۡسٌ أَوۡ فِسۡقًا أُهِلَّ لِغَيۡرِ ٱللَّهِ بِهِۦۚ فَمَنِ
ٱضۡطُرَّ غَيۡرَ بَاغٖ وَلَا عَادٖ فَإِنَّ رَبَّكَ غَفُورٞ رَّحِيمٞ﴾

> *Say, ⌜O Prophet,⌝ "I do not find in what has been revealed to me anything forbidden to eat except carrion, running blood, swine—which is impure—or a sinful offering in the name of any other than Allah. But if someone is compelled by necessity—neither driven by desire nor exceeding immediate need—then surely your Lord is All-Forgiving, Most Merciful."* [6:145]

God draws our intention to its impurity to instill certainty in us that Islam is keen to preserve our health. Dr. Ahmad Shawqi al-Fanjari presented his research titled *al-Asbāb al-'Ilmiyyah li Taḥreem laḥm al-Khinzeer* (Medical Explanations for the Prohibition of Pork), wherein he proved that pork can contain tapeworms, which can travel from the meat to the organs of the one who ate it, and pierce it, entering into the blood circulation. If it reaches the brain, it can cause brain damage, paralysis, or brain seizures. If it reaches the eye, it can cause blindness, and if it reaches the heart, it can cause a heart attack. The World Health Organization announced that their researchers in Denmark found that pork is most highly vulnerable to contamination. They found that at least 40% of pork meat carried both infectious and non-infectious microbes.

Something else to note is that zoologists categorize pigs as carnivores (like lions, wolves, foxes, and dogs) because of their canine teeth. Pigs have four large canine teeth, and Islam forbids eating any predator with canines and birds with talons.[1] Eating these animals, as research confirms, makes one more aggressive and violent. In countries where cock-fighting is a common sport, it was found that those who breed chickens for fighting feed them meat instead of fodder so that they would behave more aggressively and be ready to kill. It is known that pigs are more vicious and harsh than sheep and cows, which eat grass. Female pigs are commonly afflicted with aggressive behavior after giving birth, called savaging, and are prone to kill and eat their own offspring. This is why pig herders are forced to remove the canines of the pigs when they are young so that they do not attack their offspring when they grow. It is also found that when the pigs in Europe and America leave their clean pens and go off to the forests, they quickly revert to eating dead mice and animal carcasses.

The fat of pork contains complex fats like triglycerides

1 al-Bukhari and at-Tirmidhi report from Ibn 'Abbas that the Messenger of Allah ﷺ forbade eating any fanged predator and every bird with a talon. For more, refer to *Nayl al-Awṭār* by ash-Shawkāni.

and contains fifteen times the amount of cholesterol than beef. Pork is significantly higher in fat than beef. Such high fat content causes clogged arteries and a high risk of heart disease, which is the number one killer in the west. The disease of influenza first appeared among pig farmers. It then spread to those who ate the pigs, and was thus called Swine Flu. It spread worldwide, and there is still no doctor who could find a cure for the root of the disease.

The negative effects of different foods and hygiene habits are still being researched and discovered by health experts. Islam, in its mercy and compassion, gives Muslim an early immunization against disease and bacteria, and arms them with daily default measures to protect their bodies against harm. By following God's guidance, instead of relying on the often-changing and haphazard progress of health research, the purification rituals and guidelines in Islam keep us one step ahead.

## Prayer

Prayer is, at its root, worship performed by the soul, a spiritual act, but it is also a means of training our character, mind, and body. Prayer is a form of physical exercise. When you wake up for the Fajr prayer, breathe in the fresh morning air, and walk to the mosque with motivation and lofty aspirations, remember the following hadith in which the Prophet ﷺ said, *"Give the good news of a complete light on the Day of Resurrection to those who walk to the mosque in the dark."*[1]

1 *Sunan Ibn Majah:* The Book on Mosques, "Walking to Prayer," #780

Imagine walking to the mosque for every prayer; and then standing and sitting therein, perfecting your posture; bowing down straight to strengthen your legs, hands, and back; and then maintaining the correct position in your prostration. This daily routine keeps your body strong and agile. And while the heart feels weak and broken in front of its Creator, the limbs are not to display this. When Umar saw a man feigning weakness in prayer, he said to him, "You will kill our religion for us—may God destroy you!" He saw another man hanging his neck low while standing as a display of humility, but he told him, "Raise your head! Humility comes from the heart, not the neck."

When your love for worship reaches a certain level, you begin to prefer standing for long periods in front of God over sleeping at night. You wake up in the middle of the night, as God says:

﴿تَتَجَافَىٰ جُنُوبُهُمْ عَنِ ٱلْمَضَاجِعِ يَدْعُونَ رَبَّهُمْ خَوْفًا
وَطَمَعًا وَمِمَّا رَزَقْنَـٰهُمْ يُنفِقُونَ ۞ فَلَا تَعْلَمُ نَفْسٌ مَّآ
أُخْفِىَ لَهُم مِّن قُرَّةِ أَعْيُنٍ جَزَآءًۢ بِمَا كَانُوا۟ يَعْمَلُونَ﴾

*They abandon their beds, invoking their Lord with hope and fear, and donate from what We have provided for them. No soul can imagine what delights are kept in store for them as a reward for what they used to do.*
[34:16-17]

Standing in prayer at night, humbling yourself to your Lord and breaking into tears in front of Him actually gives the body strength and fortitude. It cleanses the eye of any filth and the heart of any hardness, and it helps the body escape its habits of laziness and lethargy. That is why the Prophet ﷺ said,

> *Satan ties three knots in the nape of your neck while you sleep, saying with each knot, 'You have such a long night ahead of you, so sleep.' Then when you wake up and remember Allah, one knot comes undone. Then when you make wuḍu', another knot comes undone. Then when you pray, another knot comes undone, and you become energetic and positive. Otherwise, you wake up feeling disturbed and lazy.*[1]

This hadith shows the difference between one who prays and one who does not. The former is energetic and pleasant, while the latter is lazy and disturbed inside. Every Muslim should follow the first example, which earns the love of God and His Messenger.

### Prayer engages the body

The rules and movements of prayer prepare the body in the best of ways for self-development. Physical fitness used to only be seen as an engagement of the body, not the soul. Shaykh Amin al-Khouli says: "The concept of physical fitness is now more general and inclusive. It now incorporates the wellness of the body and the soul." He shows the effect of the prayer's combination of both of these components, saying, "Through the obligation to pray, the human being conditions both his soul and his body. God,

1 *Sahih al-Bukhari:* The Book on Jihad, "Satan's Knots on the Nape of the Neck of One who Does Not Pray at Night" #1142

in all His wisdom, obligated the human being to pray, simultaneously combining spiritual humility with physical activity."

Dr. al-Khouli also mentions the movements of prayer—standing, bowing, prostrating, and then standing up again, in addition to turning the face right and left at the end of the prayer—all comprise bodily movements that one should not neglect. Experts in natural medicine affirm that all of these movements help to maintain and activate the muscle tone, keeping the range of flexibility for the major muscles—namely, those that help keep the human being standing straight. Any weakness in any of these body parts may subject it to deformation, which can then impede upon one's quality of life.

By walking to the mosque daily, in addition to the actual prayer that we perform, we would go even further in preserving our physical fitness to the standards necessary for maintaining good health. Not only would it preserve our physical strength, but also our flexibility and ability in the muscles and joints used for prayer in a timely, wholesome, and disciplined manner.[1]

## Physical accommodations in prayer

The rules of the prayer all take into consideration the physical differences of all Muslims. Someone who is physically ill is not required to stand up for prayer, as someone who is healthy would normally be required to do. Someone who is unable to stand may pray sitting down, lying down, or even

1 *ar-Riyāḍah wal-Ḥiḍarah al-Islāmiyyah,* p. 73

by indicating the movements of prayer by gesturing with their head. Someone who is exhausted by travel is even permitted to shorten and combine their prayers.

It is the Prophetic tradition to delay the prayer until cooler hours in severe heat, and in severe weather people are encouraged to pray in their houses rather than in the mosque. Abdullah bin Umar narrates that when the Messenger of Allah ﷺ announced that prayer be held in the houses on a rainy, cold, and windy night.[1] This was so that no one slips and harms themselves. The Prophet ﷺ also prohibited praying all night without sleep, and warned Abdullah bin 'Amr against this. He asked him, *"I was informed that you fast all day and pray all night."* He replied: "That is correct, O Messenger of Allah." He warned: *"Don't. Fast one day, and eat another. Pray, and also sleep. Your body has a right over you, your health has a right over you, your wife has a right over you, and your visitors have a right over you."*[2]

We can see how the Prophet ﷺ gave the body its proper attention, as opposed to only being concerned with the soul at the body's expense. After all, we use our body to perform our worship. Imam al-Bukhari named a chapter in his book after this phenomenon: "Going to Extremes in Worship is Disliked." It is a great resource for studying the hadiths regarding physical discipline and fitness. Similarly, Shaykh Amin al-Khouli named a chapter in his book *ar-Riyāḍah wal-Ḥaḍārah al-Islāmiyyah* (*Exercise in Islamic society*),

1 al-Bukhari, *Sahih al-Bukhari:* The Book on Adhan, "Concessions in Rain," #1116

2 *Sahih al-Bukhari:* The Book on Fasting, "The Fast of David," # 1979

"Balancing the Soul and the Body," and in it he shows that rest is an essential part of physical fitness. Fatigue causes physical illness and tension, and strains the body. There has even recently appeared the concept of regulated rest, which is now a part of physical fitness.

There are different types of rest. There is passive rest, like sleep and relaxation, and there is active rest, like resting some muscles and working out others. Everybody has physical limits that they must not overstep, as shown in the hadith of Abdullah bin 'Amr bin Amr. This "recent" concept for physical discipline is affirmed by all of the Islamic rulings for worship, especially prayer. Even the Messenger of Allah ﷺ was commanded to give his body proper sleep. God said:

﴿يَـٰٓأَيُّهَا ٱلْمُزَّمِّلُ ۞ قُمِ ٱلَّيْلَ إِلَّا قَلِيلًا﴾

*O you wrapped ⌜in your clothes⌝! Stand all night ⌜in prayer⌝ except a little* [73:1-2]

He also says:

﴿وَمِنَ ٱلَّيْلِ فَتَهَجَّدْ بِهِۦ نَافِلَةً لَّكَ﴾

*And rise at ⌜the last⌝ part of the night, offering additional prayers...* [17:79]

Notice how God commanded him to pray "part of the night," and not all of it.

There is also active rest, which is to rest some muscles while using others. For example, one who prays sitting down must still perform the other moves of prayer. Another example is the different ways of sitting in the *tashahhud* of the prayer. Islam's excellence really shows the difference between its form of spirituality and that of the monks, who neglect their bodies in what they deem to be worship. There are stories of monks who stood on one leg for three years straight as a form of worship, neither sleeping nor sitting for that entire period of time, only reclining his back on a stone whenever he would get tired.

### Prayer and food

Islam's concern for our physical well-being can also be seen in the hadith wherein Anas bin Malik narrates that the Prophet ﷺ said: *"When dinner is ready and the call to prayer is made, then begin with dinner."* Ibn Umar also narrates in another narration that the Prophet ﷺ forbade rushing a meal in order to catch the prayer. We see here that the approach of Islam takes into consideration the human's physical concerns that would ruin his focus in prayer, weaken his spiritual resolve, and make his mind preoccupied. When food is ready for you and you're appetite is raging, then you should not only eat your meal first, but also take your time and enjoy it.

### The timings of prayer

Professor Muhammad Kamil Abdul-Samad writes that the prayer times are the most perfect times for physical activity. The Fajr prayer is when the weather is soothing and refreshing; the Dhuhr prayer comes when the body needs to shake off its sleepiness and is most in need of restoring its balance and strength; the Maghrib time prayer prepares us to re-energize for the rest of the night; and the Isha prayer provides the body with the replenishment that it requires.

Professor Abdul-Samad mentions numerous studies in which experts affirm the various bodily benefits of prayer, such as renewing the blood circulation throughout the body. It also protects the spine by requiring that we stand up straight. One famous French orthopedic expert saw how the Muslims in Egypt were praying. He prescribed these movements to his patients, and all of the results showed improvement.

It has also been found that bowing and prostrating strengthen our back and abdomen muscles. These movements remove the fat that builds up on the wall of the stomach and help prevent abdominal distention. Prostrating also strengthens the thighs and shins, and helps extend the blood circulation to the extremities of the body. It activates the movement of the organs and works out the diaphragm.

Praying before eating helps prevent stomach ailments, because resting the nerves lowers blood pressure. The prayer also protects against mental disorders. Dr. Thomas Howe writes that the most essential component to sleeping well is prayer, as it is the most effective way to bring tranquility to the soul and rest to the nerves.

Prayer also helps soothe symptoms of incurable diseases. One doctor and professor writes that there are thousands of conditions that the best doctors and most qualified experts in the world have no clue how to cure. But we know that they are not insurmountable, and a miraculous phenomenon called prayer seems to break through to the cure in some cases. Dr. Alexis Carrel, surgeon, biologist, and Nobel prize laureate, wrote, "As a physician, I have seen men, after all other therapy had failed, lifted out of disease and melancholy by the serene effort of prayer. It is the only power in the world that seems to overcome the so-called laws of nature; the occasions on which prayer has dramatically done this have been termed miracles... The words, "Ask and it shall be given to you," have been verified by the experience of humanity. True, prayer may not restore the dead child to life or bring relief from physical pain. But prayer, like radium, is a source of luminous, self-generating energy."[1] Prayer has a medicinal nature, and we have seen it successful in curing illnesses such as tuberculosis, arthritis, and cancer.[2]

I find myself in complete agreement with Alija Izzetbegović, a leading Muslim intellectual and the first president of Bosnia, when he points out that prayer is not limited to being an intellectual and spiritual act of worship, but also includes a physical component. There is more to it than just mystical contemplation; it includes practical physical work as well. There is a sense of military discipline to making *wuḍu'* with cold water in the early morning and lining up in orderly ranks. This could not be overlooked by one of the officers in the Persian army before the battle of Qādisiyyah. He saw the army lined up in ranks for the Fajr prayer, and said to his commander, "Look at the Muslim army! They are starting their daily military drills!" The bodily movements in prayer are simple—to a certain extent—but involve almost all of the body's muscles. The five prayers,

1 Alexis Carrel. "The Power of Prayer" *The Reader's Digest.* (March 1941)

2 Muhammad Kamil Abdul-Ṣamad, *al-I'jāz al-'Ilmi fil-Islām*, pp. 23-25; see also al-Qaradawi, *al-'Ibādah fil-Islām*, p. 232

along with *wuḍu'* and bathing are practical ways to combat laziness and lethargy.

## ZAKAH

At its surface, the benefits of Zakah seem to be limited to our spirituality, character, and economy, but a closer look will reveal that there are many ways in which Zakah actually takes into consideration our physical component.

### ZAKAH AND BASIC HUMAN NEEDS

There is a minimum threshold that must be met for every type of wealth that Zakah is due upon. Abu Sa'eed al-Khudri narrates that the Messenger of Allah ﷺ said: *"There is no Zakah due on less than five camels. There is no Zakah due on less than five Uqiyyah of silver. There is no Zakah due on less than five wasq of dates."*[1] This threshold ensures that we have a reasonable amount of food to sustain ourselves. God says,

﴿إِنَّ لَكَ أَلَّا تَجُوعَ فِيهَا وَلَا تَعْرَىٰ
وَأَنَّكَ لَا تَظْمَؤُا فِيهَا وَلَا تَضْحَىٰ﴾

*Here it is guaranteed that you will never go hungry or unclothed, nor will you ⌜ever⌝ suffer from thirst or ⌜the sun's⌝ heat."* [20:118-119]

1 [**Translator's Note**]: The Uqiyyah was a common unit of measurement for silver. The *wasq* was a common unit of measurement for dates, equivalent to about 200 liters according to some scholars.

These principles help ensure that we never go hungry, naked, or thirsty, and that we never sleep or spend the day unclothed. We should have shelter to protect us from the rain and the heat. All of these are physical needs that Islam obligates us to secure for ourselves. Zakah is not obligatory until these bare necessities are obtained.

This minimum threshold is called the *niṣāb*. It is a means of honoring the physical needs of human beings, as it is impermissible to delay one's attempt to secure the *niṣāb*, just as it is to neglect complying with it. Islam is distinguished and unique in how it mandates responsibility and honors the needs of all human beings, in their physical, personal, and social needs. We should be able to dress to the standards of our peers and attain the standard of living within our neighborhoods. Then, if we still have extra to surpass the minimum threshold of wealth, only then must we pay Zakah. Otherwise, it is not obligated at all.

When the world organizations tried to find a solution for this issue, they set standard wage limits for all of the nations. They set one amount for people who were single, another for those who were married, and another for those who have dependants. When they applied these to everybody universally, it ended up being a gross injustice. There were some single people who were ill and had medical expenses that were double the standard cost of living for the married person. The standards they set were not suitable for all of the various circumstances.

Islam, on the other hand, relieves us of this dilemma, as it directs us to share our wealth in a balanced way. God says,

﴿وَٱلَّذِينَ إِذَآ أَنفَقُواْ لَمۡ يُسۡرِفُواْ وَلَمۡ يَقۡتُرُواْ
وَكَانَ بَيۡنَ ذَٰلِكَ قَوَامٗا﴾

*⌜They are⌝ those who spend neither wastefully nor stingily, but moderately in between.* [25:67]

We must pay a set percentage of any wealth in our possession for over one whole year, beyond a minimum threshold amount, preserving the human's physical needs while balancing the needs of others.

## ZAKAH AND SOCIAL RESPONSIBILITY

Anyone who does not have the basic necessities according to the customary standards of life must then be taken care of by others. Ibn Rajab says that one's home, vehicle, and even their servant, that is required to live do not count as surplus wealth that would prevent such a person from being qualified for receiving Zakah money. These things are not taken into consideration in issues like determining whether such a person can afford Hajj, or determining what kind of atonement they must pay for the sins that require offering material expiation. Such basic wealth must also not be used to repay debts. A number of scholars mention that whoever has a basic furnished house, a servant, and clothing, but is still in need of receiving Zakah, is eligible to receive it.[1]

This is of the clearest proofs that Islam upholds our

1 Ibn Qudāmah, *Al-Mughni*, v. 4, pp. 117-123; al-Jaṣṣāṣ al-Ḥanafi, *Ahkām al-Qur'an*, v. 1, p. 461; ash-Shawkāni, *Nayl al-Awṭār*, v. 4, p. 223-228; al-Qaraḍāwi, *Fiqh az-Zakāh*, v. 2, 561-563

physical well-being without any compromise. The most powerful hadith in this regard is narrated by Anas bin Malik. The Messenger of Allah ﷺ said: *"No one who sleeps with a full stomach while knowing that his neighbor to his side sleeps hungry truly believes in me."*[1] Adhering to principles like these would ensure that every naked body finds clothes, every empty stomach finds food, every dry throat finds water, and that every homeless person finds suitable housing. A poor judge may be provided housing from the Zakah treasury, and should not be forced to live in a dwelling or drive a vehicle that does not suit their societal status. Rulings like this simultaneously maintain physical and spiritual well-being.

### Financial obligation beyond Zakah

The injunction in our religion to take care of the needs of the body and the soul is not just limited to paying Zakah. It even extends to a financial obligation for the rich to take care of the poor. Ibn Hazm says that it is obligatory for the wealthy citizens of every locality to take care of their neighbors in need, and that the authorities must force them to do so if the Zakah does not suffice. The poor must be provided daily food, clothing appropriate for both the summer and winter, and dwellings that protect them from rain, heat, the rays of the sun, and the eyes of passers-by.[2]

Statements like that of Ibn Hazm and many others clearly show Islam's concern with the essential physical needs that

1 al-Munāwi, *Fayḍ al-Qadeer*, v. 5, p. 406, #7771

2 Ibn Hazm, *al-Muḥalla*, v. 7, p. 156, #725

we require for basic functionality. Seeing what the world has come to in our times, where one-third of the world's population still does not have access to proper nutrition, we must ask ourselves whether it is due to a lack of food or a lack of empathy. There are millions of Muslims and human brethren who die every year because of poverty and starvation. The newspapers remind us every day of those who are suffering in Bangladesh, Kashmir, Burma, Yemen, Syria, Somalia—and the list can go on. So many Muslims live daily with the inescapable pains of hunger or with improperly treated diseases, and they are not finding any help. How did we Muslims end up being so heartless and callous when our scriptures so heavily emphasize compassion and empathy?

Naturally what comes next is destruction. When the rich live in constant fear of being attacked by the poor, and the poor live in constant fear of being taken advantage of by the rich, there is a cold war between them that grows more dangerous every day as the disparity gets larger. Why do we live in such a disgraceful condition when God has given us so much honor? He says,

﴿وَلَقَدْ كَرَّمْنَا بَنِيٓ ءَادَمَ﴾

*Indeed, We have dignified the children of Adam…*
[17:70]

All humans, regardless of what they believe, are to be honored. Every time someone feeds a hungry person, takes care of an orphan, or helps someone who is lost and cannot find their way, it demonstrates what life should be like—a life where attention is paid to the physical needs of all. There is a well-established and unanimously agreed upon principle in our religion that makes sharing food, clothing, and shelter with those in need obligatory on those who have a surplus. If those for whom we are responsible die due to our lack of care, then we are to be held responsible for their deaths.

### Generosity extends to everyone

The spirit of Zakah in addressing the bodily and spiritual needs of a Muslim can also be seen in the economic rulings regarding non-Muslims in our religion. Umar bin al-Khattab felt grieved when saw a Jewish man begging, and so he gave him enough money to take care of himself. When Abdul-Malik bin Marwān sent al-Ḍaḥḥāk bin Abdul-Raḥmān al-Ash'ari to the Persians in order to collect the taxes from them, he calculated the yearly salary of the collector and paid for all of his expenses, including his food, drink, clothing, accommodations, and even his shoes. Umar bin al-Khattab warned his tax collectors Uthman bin Haneef and Hudhayfah bin Yaman from enforcing taxes on non-Muslims that they could not afford. The second century scholar of Shafi'i fiqh Abu 'Ubayd said that this is the correct way of collecting taxes from non-Muslims. They must only pay what they can afford to pay without any harm or burden.[1]

[1] Abu Yusuf, *al-Kharāj*, p. 41; Abu 'Ubayd, *al-Amwāl*, # 106

### CELEBRATIONS AND GIVING

The holidays in Islam are holidays of giving. This is so that no family spends the day in the distress of their poverty while those around them are celebrating extravagantly. On Eid ul-Fiṭr (The Eid of Feasting), Islam demands that the poor be given staple foods so they may enjoy full stomachs and do not have to spend the day begging. Its objective is demonstrated clearly in the hadith reported by Abu Dawud and al-Ḥākim that states that the Prophet ﷺ made Zakah al-Fiṭr mandatory in order to purify our fasting of any useless and foul speech, and in order to feed the poor.[1] This empathy even transfers from the poor Muslims to their poor non-Muslim neighbors. Abu Yusuf reports that when aḍ-Ḍaḥḥāk lowered the tax for the Persians, he allowed them to deduct their religious holiday expenditures as write-off.[2]

## FASTING

Fasting targets the soul, the character, and the body all at once, perhaps more so than any other act of worship. Below are some of effects of fasting on the health of the Muslim.

### THE SUNNAH OF SUHOOR

The pre-dawn meal, *suḥoor*, is a strongly encouraged

1 *Sunan Abu Dawud:* The Book on Zakah, "Zakah al-Fiṭr," #1543; al-Ḥākim al-Naysāboori, *al-Mustadrak 'Ala aṣ-Ṣaḥīḥayn:* The Book on Zakah, "Zakah al-Fiṭr purifies One's Fast," v. 1, p. 409

2 *al-Kharāj*, p. 41

tradition of the Prophet ﷺ (*sunnah mustaḥabbah*).[1] It is also a sunnah to delay the *suḥoor* until it is almost dawn, and some define it as the length of reciting 50 verses of the Quran.[2] Anas ibn Malik relates that the Prophet ﷺ said, *"Eat suḥoor, for there is blessing in suḥoor."*[3]

In another hadith, the Prophet ﷺ said, *"Suḥoor is blessed. Do not abandon it, even if you only take a gulp of water. Allah and His angels praise those who eat suḥoor."* Al-'Irbad bin Saryah said, "The Prophet ﷺ called me to eat *suḥoor* with him in Ramadan, saying, *'Come to the blessed meal!'*"[4]

These sayings encourage us to eat *suḥoor* even if we think we can do without it, or have no appetite in the morning. The Creator knows best that our body is in need of that nourishment, even if just a drink of water. The fact that Allah and His angels praise those who eat *suḥoor*, and that we can take some part of what the Prophet ﷺ called a "blessed meal," is even greater motivation to make the effort to wake up and eat before the fast begins.

1 [**Translator's Note**]: *Sunnah* linguistically means a way or path to follow. Here, it means the actions promoted and encouraged by the Prophet ﷺ for all of his followers.

2 *Sahih al-Bukhari*: The Book of Fasting, "The Length of Time between Suḥoor and the Fajr Prayer," # 1921; *Sahih Muslim*: The Book of Fasting, "The Benefits of Suḥoor," p. 1, p. 443

3 *Sahih Muslim*: The Book of Fasting, "The Benefits of Suḥoor," v. 1, p. 443; *Sunan Ibn Majah*: Book of Fasting, "Suḥoor," # 1692

4 *Sunan Abu Dawud*: Book of Fasting, "Calling Suḥoor 'The Blessed Meal,'" # 2244

### HASTENING TO BREAK THE FAST

The importance of caring for the body is emphasized in another sunnah of fasting: hastening to break it. Sahl bin Sa'd said that the Prophet ﷺ said, *"There is still good in people so long as they hasten to break their fast at its time."*[1] Hastening *ifṭār*, which is at sunset, and delaying *suḥoor* within their permitted time frames, keeps the length of the fast to the shortest possible time the day will allow. It is recommended to break the fast with only water and dates to restore energy and quench the thirst before one prays the Maghrib prayer.

In northern regions of the world, daylight lasts for 20 hours or longer. Muslim scholars used *ijtihad* (scholarly rigor and intellectual effort) to extract special rulings for such places so as to relieve hardship on people and not cause them undue burden. The goals of fasting is not to deprive people of their energy and vitality. According to their rulings, people living in these areas should follow the nearest area with reasonable daylight hours, using the time of their Fajr and Maghrib prayers to start and break their fasts. Such guidelines reflect the Islamic priorities of ease and alleviating difficulty on the body.

### IMPERMISSIBILITY OF CONSECUTIVE FASTS

The Prophet ﷺ forbade fasting consecutively: fasting every single day, outside of Ramadan as a lifelong practice. When Abdullah bin 'Amr attempted to practice this, the Prophet ﷺ stopped him, saying, *"If you do so, your eyes will become sunken and you will feel debilitated. Whoever fasts continuously,*

1 *al-Lu'lu' wal-Marjān*, # 667

*then their fast is not valid."*[1] Islam's priority of protecting and strengthening the body is clear in this hadith.

The Prophet ﷺ would take note of the physical strength and weakness of the companions. He encouraged them to be healthy and strong, and was concerned if he saw them appearing unusually feeble. The Prophet ﷺ once did not recognize a visitor, so the man said, "Messenger of Allah, I am the same man who came to you before!" The Prophet ﷺ asked, *"Then why are you so frail now?"* The man replied, "Messenger of Allah, I don't eat during the day; I only eat at night." The Prophet answered, *"Who told you to punish yourself?"*[2] This man had become overly enthusiastic upon accepting Islam, fasting the entire year so that his body became frail and weak, but the Prophet ﷺ rejected this practice, calling it self-punishment to show that it is outside the scope of worship. This kind of self-inflicted weakness is not part of Islam.

Fasting in its best form should, in fact, strengthen and invigorate the body. In the aforementioned hadith narrated by Abdallah bin Amr bin Al-As, the Prophet ﷺ went on to describe the characteristics of Prophet Dawud: he would fast one day, break his fast the next, and would always stand strong and firm in battle. Prophet Dawud's worship did not make him retreat from society or become frail. He was diligent in worship and brave in combat.

1 *Sahih al-Bukhari*: Book of Fasting, "The Fast of Dawud" # 1979

2 *Sunan Ibn Majah*: The Book of Fasting, # 1741

### THOSE EXCUSED FROM FASTING

The following are the categories of conditions that exclude people from fasting:[1]

1. Traveling
2. Illness
3. Young age
4. Mental disability
5. Old age
6. Being required to rescue and save a life that would be impossible when fasting
7. Being completely incapacitated by hunger and thirst
8. Being coerced to break the fast
9. Pregnancy and breastfeeding
10. Menstruation and postpartum bleeding

Ibn Al-Qayyim included among these categories fighting in the cause of Allah, because the difficulty of fighting is greater than the difficulty of travel. Ibn Al-Qayyim supported his argument with evidence that Umar allowed soldiers to break their fast upon meeting the enemy.[2]

All of these allowable conditions for breaking the fast are in line with the goal of protecting physical health. We break our fast when we travel so that we are not overly exhausted by our travels, and we break our fast when we fall ill in order to not worsen our condition or interfere with treatment. Children need regular nourishment for their growing bodies, and the elderly may have lost their

1 Fayhan al-Matiri, *Aṣ-Ṣawm wal-Ifṭār li'Aṣḥab al-Ā'thār*

2 Ibn al-Qayyim, *Zād al-Ma'ād*, v. 1, pp. 22, 222

ability to endure the physical strain of fasting. A person who faces an emergency, such as a collapsed building or a dangerous fire, may break his fast so as to be capable of saving lives. Someone who is so overcome with hunger and thirst that he or she is on the verge of losing consciousness may break the fast. People who fear persecution or death if they fast, such as those who are coerced to break their fast, are excused from fasting. Pregnant and breastfeeding women may break their fast if it may affect the feeding and nourishment of their child. Women who have their periods or are experiencing postnatal bleeding are also relieved of the added hardship of fasting.

We can see that one of the goals behind the rulings of worship is to protect the body from any harm. This priority underpins all of the rulings regarding fasting. The exclusions from fasting comprise one of the widest doors of facilitation and ease in Islamic fiqh and understanding.

### Water and dates

All of the scholars agree that the best fasting etiquette is to break the fast on dates and water. Ibn Ḥazm's view was the dates should be eaten first and then water if they are consumed together. If there are no dates, then the fast must be broken with water before any other foods.[1] The majority of scholars are of the view that the etiquette mentioned by Ibn Ḥazm is recommended but not obligatory.

Breaking the fast with dates restores the body's blood sugar levels to normal. Low blood sugar can cause a variety

1 Ibn Ḥazm, *al-Muḥalla*, v. 8, p. 31, # 806

of problems, and eating dates to break the fast replenishes sugar levels quickly. When we use other foods besides dates to break our fast, it takes our digestive system much longer to translate those foods into what our body needs. Water and dates restore the body's energy most efficiently.[1]

### Health benefits of fasting

Many Muslim researchers have studied the physical effects of fasting. In fact, experts in medicine and nutrition have become fascinated of late by the undeniable benefits of fasting on physical health.

Fasting is a detoxification process. It cleanses the blood and flushes out toxins. Because human beings have to eat every day, there is an inevitable accumulation of toxins and poisonous residue in our bodies that makes us feel lethargic. Fasting lightens our bodies and frees us from the effect of those toxins.[2] By the middle of Ramadan, we can feel a difference in our health.

Especially if we have become used to eating food as a comfort and a luxury, fasting can have a strong health impact. Many of us eat and drink for pleasure and spend much of our days seated at a desk or driving. These are damaging habits in every aspect: bad for our blood circulation, bad for our digestion, bad for our heart, and bad for our spiritual health. Fasting is a training to restore our strength. The Prophet ﷺ said, "*Fast, and you will be healthy.*"[3] Fasting one

1 al-Fanjari, *aṭ-Ṭibb Al-Waqā'ī fil-Islām*, p. 66

2 Muhammad Mahmud as-Ṣawwāf, *aṣ-Ṣiyām fil-Islām*, pp. 25-26

3 Narrated by Abu Hurayrah, authenticated by Ibn as-Sunni and Abu Nu'aym

month a year, according to experts, can rid the body of the weak and dead cells that have accumulated throughout the year.

Dr. Muhammad Ali al-Barr studied the effects of fasting on the body. He said that the food we eat goes through three phases:

1. Food is first digested and converted to necessary nutrients. The digestive system and the liver play a large part in this process. The nutrients are absorbed by the bloodstream and carried to every single cell according to its needs.
2. Extra glucose and fatty acids are then converted to fat and stored in the body in the liver and different parts of the torso.
3. When food is unavailable to the body, the adrenal glands, thyroid, pancreas, and pituitary all work together to convert the stored fats back into the glucose and fatty acids that the body needs.

When the body is fasting, it is forced to use its energy stores and eliminate cells that are dysfunctional or diseased. Fasting plays the role of targeting potential disease-causing cells of the body and purging them. It has even been observed that tumors shrink while a person is fasting. Fasting gives a break to our digestive system, allowing our stomach, liver, and intestines to rest and heal.

Fasting is also one of the best ways to combat obesity and its many associated diseases. In addition to the benefits mentioned earlier, researchers have found that fasting cleanses the body of microbes and bacterial infections. It also protects against diabetes, reduces inflammation, and prevents some types of arthritis.

# HAJJ

Hajj, like fasting, is intense both spiritually and physically. It has many profound and beneficial impacts on the body. In order to make Hajj, one first must have the means to do so. God says:

﴿وَلِلَّهِ عَلَى ٱلنَّاسِ حِجُّ ٱلْبَيْتِ مَنِ ٱسْتَطَاعَ إِلَيْهِ سَبِيلًا﴾

*Pilgrimage to this House is an obligation by Allah upon whoever is able among the people.* [3:97]

Physical ability to travel and perform the acts of Hajj must be taken into consideration when deciding whether or not someone is able to make Hajj. Ibn Hazm defines the phrase "being able to," in the verse as "being healthy and able to walk."[1] Hajj is like jihad[2] in a way. It requires physical strength in order to even complete the rituals therein.

## SAFETY ON THE JOURNEY

Before embarking on Hajj, one must also make sure that their journey will be safe so as not to be attacked by

1 *al-Muhallah*, v. 3, p. 53

2 [**Translator's note:** Jihad means striving in God's cause. It includes striving for self-improvement, striving for knowledge, striving against temptation and evil, and striving on the battlefield.]

highway robbers or criminals lying in wait to rob or capture those making pilgrimage to Allah's house. If fear of this is warranted, then one is not obliged to make Hajj, even if he could afford to and is physically able to do so. This is to preserve our physical and financial well-being.

### The importance of physical provision

A Muslim may not set out for Hajj, feeling giddy and high spirited, but without enough money for transportation, food, drink, and acommodation. Setting out with the intention of begging is not allowed either. Even if someone has enough to sustain them for the first few days, they would be subjecting their body to harm if they end up not finding what is necessary for the rest of their trip.

We saw in previous chapters that the Prophet ﷺ forbade the people of Yemen from making Hajj without any provisions. The scholars add that the minimum provisions required to make Hajj include provisions for the pilgrim himself, his family, and anyone who depends on him in his town.[1] You cannot use all of the money you have to make Hajj, leaving your family to starve and suffer; this would be a confusion of priorities, a failure to fulfill an immediate obligation in order to complete an obligation that may be performed later.

### Cleanliness During Hajj

It is *sunnah* for the one making Hajj or Umrah to shave

1 Ibn al-Hammām, *Sharḥ Fatḥ al-Qadeer,* v. 1, p. 418; Ibn Qudāmah, *al-Mughni*

their pubic and underarm hair, clip their nails, trim their mustache, and bathe and apply perfume before entering the state of *iḥrām*.[1] It is also *sunnah* to remove any dirt and bathe once you enter Mecca, while performing *ṭawāf*, and upon entering Mina and 'Arafah. All of these rulings during Hajj show the importance of self-grooming. We also learn from the Sunnah to change our clothing whenever they get dirty, keeping the Muslims in a state of cleanliness and distinguishing them from others.

All of this indicates that in being fully invested in one's spiritual pursuits, one must not be too preoccupied to tend to their physical hygiene. The link between the body and the soul is firm and strong. If you do not bathe before making *ṭawāf*, you may disrupt the humble and pious focus of those around you by making them smell your foul odors. Not to mention that you will be moving around a lot, covered in dust and sweat, during the rituals in Hajj. This may lead to blockage of the sweat glands on your body and cause illness.

## Sickness and Hajj

A ruling of Hajj that demonstrates very clearly Islam's emphasis on public health is that it prioritizes the wellbeing of the group over the individual obligation to perform Hajj. If someone has a contagious disease, then this removes from them the obligation to make Hajj so as not to infect

1 [**Translator's Note**]: The word *sunnah* with a small "*s*" indicates that something is encouraged and recommended in the religion, and is in accordance with the Prophet's teaching. The word Sunnah with a capital "S" refers to the overall teachings of the Prophet ﷺ.

others. We can find this gem in a narration reported by Imam Malik from Ibn Abu Ma'bad. Umar bin al-Khattab passed by a woman suffering from leprosy (a contagious skin disease) near the Kaaba and said: "Do not harm the people; go stay in your house." She stayed at home, and when a man passed by her after that, he said: "The man who forbade you from coming out has died, so come out." She said: "I would never obey him while he is alive and then disobey while he is dead."[1]

Umar's words embody the spirit of our religious law. This explains why the woman obeyed the command even after he died, expecting a reward from Allah for doing so. This story provides for us a beautiful example, both in the ruling issued by Umar and in the woman's willingness to comply, which is unheard of in our modern times.

### Accommodation in Hajj rulings

If one's illness is not contagious, then they may make Hajj as long as they are able to complete the rituals. But Islam goes even further to make the rituals easy for those who are sick. This is a display of God's compassion towards us.

One example is found in *Sahih al-Bukhari*. Umm Salamah narrates that she complained to the Messenger of Allah ﷺ that she was feeling ill. He said: *"Perform ṭawāf behind everyone else while riding."*[2] Aishah also narrates that when they were staying overnight in Muzdalifah, Sawdah asked the Prophet ﷺ if she could leave before the stampede of

1 *Al-Muwaṭṭa'*, "Gathering for Hajj," vol. 1, p. 424

2 *Sahih al-Bukhari:* The Book on Hajj, "Allowing Women and the Weak to Leave Muzdalifah Early," #1633

people. She was a slow woman, so he permitted her, and she left before the stampede. Ibn 'Abbas also narrates that he was among those whom the Prophet ﷺ sent out on the night of Muzdalifa with the weak ones in his family.

Another example is that someone with a disease on their scalp may shave their head early. Ka'b bin Umar narrates, "When I came to the Messenger of Allah, lice was scattered all over my face. He said: *'I did not know that it would be this difficult for you. Could you find sheep?'* I said, 'No,' so he said: *'Fast three days or feed six poor people half of a ṣā' of food each, and shave your head.'* The ayahs came down about me specifically, but apply for you all." He was speaking about the ayah:

﴿وَلَا تَحۡلِقُواْ رُءُوسَكُمۡ حَتَّىٰ يَبۡلُغَ ٱلۡهَدۡيُ مَحِلَّهُۥۚ فَمَن
كَانَ مِنكُم مَّرِيضًا أَوۡ بِهِۦٓ أَذٗى مِّن رَّأۡسِهِۦ فَفِدۡيَةٞ مِّن
صِيَامٍ أَوۡ صَدَقَةٍ أَوۡ نُسُكٖ﴾

*And do not shave your heads until the sacrificial animal reaches its destination. But if any of you is ill or has a scalp ailment ⌜requiring shaving⌝, then compensate either by fasting, charity, or a sacrificial offering.*
[2:297]

Rulings like these show how the rulings of Hajj take people's physical conditions into account. Someone who falls ill during the journey of Hajj may perform *ṭawāf* and *sa'y* riding on an animal (or, for example, in a wheelchair). Those who fear any harm for themselves, their womenfolk, or their children may pelt stones at the largest pelting station before Fajr as Asmā' did, or before sunrise as Sawdah and

Ibn 'Abbās did—they may even do it after the sunset, as Umm Salamah did. All of these rulings revolve around the same objective: not overburdening the Muslims above their physical capacity.

### The physical intensity of Hajj

Hajj is by far the most physically intense act of worship. Pilgrims must travel to Mecca, and then walk to the Holy Mosque and enter it to walk around the Kaaba seven times. Then they walk to the well of Zamzam, and after drinking a few sips, they climb Mount Safa, walking between it and Mount Marwah seven times (running lightly is even encouraged in certain spots on the track). They travel from Mecca to Mina, and then set out for 'Arafah, and after that Muzdalifah. After spending the night in the open desert, the Hajj pilgrims go to the largest pelting station to throw their stones, and then to the Kaaba to make *ṭawāf* once again. They return to Mina and stay there for three nights, walking quite a distance to the stations to pelt the stones every day.

These are long distances that the Hajj pilgrims often spend walking as opposed to riding in vehicles. Walking is one of the most important physical activities in preserving physical wellness. When we consider that the blessed city of Mecca is one of intense desert heat, you can imagine how intense of a workout Hajj can be for the body. It not only builds strength and endurance, but also forces the pilgrim to work up a sweat and purge their bodies of toxins.

Islam still grants those who have the financial capability, but not the physical strength, a chance to not be deprived of its reward so as not to feel like their physical condition is a hindrance to coming closer to Allah: they may send others to make Hajj in their place. This is made clear in the hadith wherein someone asked the Prophet ﷺ during his Farewell Pilgrimage, "O Messenger of Allah, Allah's duty upon His servants is Hajj, but now my father is an old man, and he cannot sit up straight on a riding animal. Will it suffice if I perform Hajj for him?" The Prophet ﷺ responded: *"Yes."*[1]

Islam clearly takes into serious consideration our physical well-being, in addition to the other *tarbiya* and developmental goals of spirituality, character, and understanding. It does not burden anyone beyond their capacity, nor does it deprive anyone who is unable to perform an act of worship from its reward.

1 'Abdul-Bāqi, *al-Lu'lu' wal-Marjān:* The Book on Hajj, "Making Hajj on Behalf of Those Who Cannot," #844

# Conclusion

Islamic worship is tailored to interact with the human soul, character, mind, and body, shaping the *tarbiya* of individuals and communities in a balanced way. Each act of worship has an active effect and a unique imprint on our development.

The human self was created in need of worship; a need as profound as our need for food, water and air. We require its balanced tempering of personality, understanding, and community in order to fulfill the mission for which we were created. The Muslim who fasts but does not pray, gives charity but does not purify the body, not only fails to deliver what is due to God, but also fails to balance and complete their own self.

Through these powerful basics of Islamic practice, individuals within the Muslim *ummah* and community take on a shared vibrancy. They bow in prayer in unison and pay a similar Zakah percentage. But more remarkably, their characters, souls, minds, and bodies are forged by the same forces, shaped by the same *tarbiya* effects of worship. By reviving the spirit and understanding inherent within worship rituals, we can restore vibrancy to the *ummah*. We become advocates of purity and cleanliness, guardians of our prayer habit, role models with luminous faces and hearts, generous character, keen insight, energetic bodies, and manners finely rendered.

This holistic understanding of the acts of worship should assume its deserved place in the strategies and programming of institutes, organizations, schools, conferences, and mosques. We must focus on nurturing the inner wellbeing of people and not merely addressing externalities. Acts of worship are *tarbiya and* training for the upcoming generations, nurturing a strength of will, sincerity in Islamic work, patience, and enduring commitment. Incorporating this dynamic understanding of worship has implications not just in the content of our programs, but also in how they are implemented.

Fiqh instruction in schools, educational institutions and curriculum design should present fiqh rulings with their *tarbiya* effects and their practical impact on the individual's life. In this way, the teacher and student interact with the knowledge at a deeper level, yielding practical results in emotions, behavior, and understanding, and not just an increase in technical knowledge or a successful course completion. By revealing the wisdom and effects of worship, we equip a generation to respond to attacks and controversy regarding specific aspects of religion. Conveying the transformative effects of Islamic worship can also become a powerful perspective in inviting people to Islam. This field of study is vast, full of undiscovered insight and potential. I encourage organizations and institutions to motivate young Muslims to explore the effects of worship in their lives and to continue this research.

# About the Author

Dr. Salah Soltan is a world-renowned Muslim scholar who resided in the United States in the nineties and early 2000's. He wrote more than 60 books in the areas of jurisprudence, family law, and other fields of Islamic knowledge. While in the United States, Dr. Soltan founded the Islamic American University, sat on the board of the Fiqh Council of North America, and lectured students around the country. He is a beloved teacher, father, and friend to many.

In his later years in the U.S., Salah Soltan was targeted by an Islamophobic smear campaign. He relocated to Bahrain where he served as advisor to the Minister of Islamic Affairs. In 2012, Soltan was appointed the position of deputy minister of Islamic Affairs in Egypt. In the aftermath of the 2013 military coup, he was arrested on falsified charges and sentenced to life in prison. The U.N. committee on arbitrary detention named Salah Soltan a political prisoner and demands his immediate release.